Third Edition

Positive Classroom Management

Treat a classroom full of inner-city kids like a bunch of
uneducable future criminals, and they won't let you down.
Treat them with love, respect, and dignity, however, and watch them bloom.

—Sy Fliegel, *Miracle in East Harlem*

Remember that students will rise to meet your expectations, yes,
but also remember to rise to meet your students' and parents' expectations, too.

—Flora Gigante

Third Edition

Positive Classroom Management

A Step-by-Step Guide to Helping Students Succeed

Robert C. Di Giulio

CORWIN PRESS
A SAGE Publications Company
Thousand Oaks, CA 91320

For information:

Corwin Press
A Sage Publications Company
2455 Teller Road
Thousand Oaks, California 91320
www.corwinpress.com

Sage Publications Ltd.
1 Oliver's Yard
55 City Road
London EC1Y 1SP
United Kingdom

Sage Publications India Pvt. Ltd.
B-42, Panchsheel Enclave
Post Box 4109
New Delhi 110 017 India

Library of Congress Cataloging-in-Publication Data

Di Giulio, Robert C., 1949-
Positive classroom management : a step-by-step guide to helping students succeed / Robert C. Di Giulio. — 3rd ed.
    p. cm.
Includes bibliographical references and index.
ISBN 1-4129-3726-4 (cloth) or 978-1-412937-26-9
ISBN 1-4129-3727-2 (pbk.) or 978-1-412937-27-6
    1. Classroom management—United States. I. Title.

LB3013.D54 2007
371.102′4—dc22

2006026357

This book is printed on acid-free paper.

06 07 08 09 10 10 9 8 7 6 5 4 3 2 1

Acquisitions Editor:	Faye Zucker
Editorial Assistant:	Gem Rabanera
Production Editor:	Jenn Reese
Copy Editor:	Rachel Keith
Typesetter:	C&M Digitals (P) Ltd.
Proofreader:	Caryne Brown
Indexer:	Judy Hunt
Cover Designer:	Michael Dubowe
Graphic Designer:	Lisa Riley

Contents

Preface

Teachers need help. They want help, too. But they need and want the right kind of help. Over my 35 years as an educator, I have seen how well we teachers respond to help that is constructive, supportive, clear, and doable. This is especially true today. Our society—and our teachers—face challenges that were once not even imaginable. More strongly than ever, society is asking us to teach all students (advantaged and disadvantaged alike) to learn not simply facts but how to behave in a civilized, caring way and realize their potential as adults. To accomplish this, society has given us classroom space, some lined paper, a few computers, and little else in addressing the enormous job it has asked us to do.

About 25 years ago, as a new principal seeking to help my teachers get a handle on classroom management, I found few resources on the subject. In response, I developed and taught a course for my staff and the Vermont State College system called Managing and Understanding Children's Behavior. Since then I have continued to develop and bring together ideas and materials to help teachers create and maintain a positive classroom.

In 1995 I wrote *Positive Classroom Management*, which has been well received among colleges, in teacher preparation programs, and, most important, by teachers both new and experienced who have said how helpful they found my book. In writing this third edition, I have made changes that I believe make PCM even more useful. Of course, my emphasis is still on creating a positive classroom: on running the show without destroying student dignity.

Yes, today there are many books and resources that address control in the classroom, stating ways to "get" students to behave. What makes PCM different is that it looks past the "I win, you lose" struggle to control students and goes directly to what lies at the heart of a successful classroom. It goes past the threats, blame, rules, rewards, punishments, complaints, and excuses, all of which are residue from attempts by teachers to gain control of a classroom (usually after it is out of control). PCM highlights what effective teachers know after years of experience: It's not about achieving control but about creating caring—caring for others, caring for oneself, and caring about learning. Certainly, students need limits and structure, but they need them to be communicated within a person-to-person, proactive, real, and safe environment. Students hear and internalize teachers' expectations not through schemes or threats, but by virtue of basic understandings developed cooperatively between teachers and students. Students flourish in classrooms where they feel valued, cared for, and safe, as well as where there is challenge, curiosity, and activity. Thus, PCM is not a bag of discipline tricks: It does not advocate manipulation, getting students to obey, or securing compliance at any cost. PCM is, I believe, an honest guide to helping you create your positive classroom, not only for your survival as a teacher but also for the benefit of your students and, yes, for the benefit of the community, state, and nation.

In light of today's emphasis in our public schools upon standardized tests that measure mostly narrow and low-level skills, the real work for us teachers—the good fight—lies in helping students become successful learners, and not simply within the confines of the school or classroom. In its broadest sense, this implies the development of what Daniel Goleman calls *emotional intelligence*, the type of intelligence "it takes to lead life successfully" (1995, p. 43). Emotional intelligence, also known as one's EQ (emotional quotient), is contrasted with IQ (intelligence quotient), the traditional but limited measure of intelligence. Citing the work of several research psychologists, Goleman points to five domains of EQ, namely, "knowing one's emotions, managing emotions, motivating oneself, recognizing emotions in others, and handling relationships." Central to these domains is the development of *empathy*, which Goleman calls "the fundamental 'people skill'" because it attunes us "to the subtle social signals that indicate what others need or want" (p. 43), and which then lead "to caring, altruism, and compassion" (1995, pp. 284–285). My work and research have brought me to the same two conclusions: EQ and empathy lie at the heart of human development, and together they underpin a positive classroom. Of course, schools must teach content knowledge and application, but only a person whose senses are glued shut could deny the importance of building our students' emotional intelligence and developing their powers of empathy.

Yes, but are we teachers up to this double challenge?

My question was answered in the responses I received from 105 teachers selected by the University of Vermont for their effective teaching and commitment to children and adolescents (Di Giulio, 1994). I contacted each of these successful teachers and asked them to describe how they ran their classrooms. How, I asked, do teachers instill good behavior? More centrally, do teachers really believe in empathy? We know how easy it is to teach and learn violence, but can students be taught how to act in empathic ways toward others? Almost to a person, their answers were yes, all students should—and could—learn good behavior. Furthermore, teachers spoke of the responsibility for action on their part. Not one of the 105 teachers blamed parents; not one teacher blamed students. Instead, this group held that teachers *could* teach, *should* teach, and—in their cases—*were* teaching students positive, empathic behavior, enabling them to lead successful social and emotional lives and to be part of the social and emotional lives of others.

Yes, working toward that goal is an important use of our time, energy, and resources. The way we carry out our job—the way we manage (teach, set up, lead, care for, protect) our classrooms—determines how successful we and our students—and our society—will be. My purpose in writing this book is to provide all teachers with concrete, practical, step-by-step guidance on creating and maintaining a classroom that fosters both student scholarship and civil behavior, using an approach that is upbeat and constructive rather than negative and punitive. Helping students develop their emotional intelligence is a formidable task, given our society's emphasis on conformity, consistency, and compliance. Thus my book is about a lot more than classroom management. It is about creating a *positive classroom* and making it work. Although most of my illustrations are geared toward elementary, middle school, and high school teachers, there is much here for early childhood teachers, preschool teachers, and, I daresay, even instructors in postsecondary schools. A positive classroom benefits all students, preschool through college.

Since the first edition of this book appeared in 1995 and the second in 2000, I have received feedback from hundreds of teachers, student teachers, administrators, students, and even parents, all of which I have taken seriously. I am excited to include many updates in this third edition, including useful new concepts like the spiritual dimension, which joins the physical, instructional, and managerial dimensions. This edition provides more focus on the connection between differentiated instruction and the positive classroom, as well as greater attention to emotional intelligence, attribution teaching, and informal and formative assessments, and the checklists have been improved. I believe all of this makes the book even more user-friendly and helpful.

The Introduction looks at why positive classrooms are necessary, describing the benefits of an affirmative environment and approach to teaching students. Part I highlights how the most common types of rules work against our students' learning and developing their EQ, while proactive rules can actually help teach. Part I also introduces basic understandings, which form the bond present in all thriving classrooms.

Part II looks in depth at the four dimensions of positive classrooms. The spiritual dimension speaks to what it is like to be a student in a caring, success-oriented classroom. The physical dimension focuses on how the setup of the classroom provides a safe and productive learning environment, and the instructional dimension describes how teachers can best teach so that students are successful learners. Finally, the managerial dimension examines the noninstructional but essential routines and procedures basic to a smooth-running classroom.

Within each dimension are three types of teacher interventions, each keyed to when the intervention occurs: Preventive interventions occur before the fact and prior to teacher-student interactions, supportive interventions happen in-the-moment as instruction is taking place, and corrective interventions are made after the fact in response to something that has already happened. Preventive and supportive interventions are *proactive*, while corrective interventions are by necessity *reactive*. All teachers will at times find themselves needing to carry out corrective interventions, but Corrective City is no place to set down roots ("I'm only visiting, thank you"). We teachers do our best work when we are proactive rather than reactive.

Part III offers a blueprint for success using systematic preparation and reflection. A comprehensive summary of key points, provided in the form of step-by-step checklists, is included to help teachers create their positive classroom dimension by dimension. These checklists can be used by new teachers first entering the empty classroom weeks before the students arrive, and by experienced teachers who want to review, evaluate, or more closely examine their practices. I conclude with a guide to reflection: immediate, short-term, and long-term. Systematic reflection is essential to maintaining a positive classroom once it has been established.

This book is written for all teachers, experienced and inexperienced, veteran and student. Creating and maintaining a positive classroom not only works to the benefit of all students but also helps each of us become the best teacher possible. And it helps make teaching the satisfying and rewarding profession it should be.

Acknowledgments

Several kind experts—experienced teachers and teacher educators in the trenches—generously furnished useful suggestions as I prepared the first edition: Jennifer G. Harvey, teacher and member of the multiage team at the Crabapple Middle School in Roswell, Georgia; T. Paulette Quarrell, teacher of sixth-grade social studies and English at Deming Junior High School in Deming, New Mexico; Professor John McFadden in the Department of Teacher Education at California State University in Sacramento; Karleen Hamilton, who teaches at the El Rancho Structured School in Camarillo, California; and Chris Jakicic, principal of Willow Grove Elementary School in Buffalo Grove, Illinois.

Thoughtful advice was provided by Trish Mularchuk, a dear friend and master teacher. Trish was an exceptional teacher of exceptional education at MILA Elementary School in Merritt Island, Florida. I miss her wisdom and her friendship, but not more than her students and school community miss her smile and enduring love of teaching.

I wish to thank the following reviewers for helping me make the second edition an even better book: Susan Hansen, extension educator at the University of Nebraska—Lincoln in Schuyler, Nebraska; JoAnn Hohenbrink, assistant professor at Ohio Dominican College in Columbus, Ohio; Suzanne Schwartz McCotter, PhD candidate in middle school education at the University of Georgia in Athens, Georgia; and Dr. Brooks Aylor, assistant professor at La Salle University in Philadelphia, Pennsylvania.

I continue to appreciate my connection with Corwin Press, a most professional publishing house. From the beginning, editor Ann McMartin was a delight to work with. She gave clear and intelligent feedback on my original manuscript, and she handled matters with grace and dispatch.

I also appreciate the professional work of S. Marlene Head, Toby Hopstone, Susan McElroy, Kylee Leigl, and Gem Rabanera. Robb Clouse and Jay Whitney skillfully guided me through the second edition, and it was a stroke of luck to work with Faye Zucker, executive editor at Corwin Press, an author's gem and the guiding force behind this third edition. Her wisdom, wit, and supportive demeanor made her great to work with (and a lot of fun to have lunch with). I could not have asked for better fortune than to work with production editor Jenn Reese and copy editor Rachel Keith. Their knowledgeable recommendations and sharp eyes helped make this third edition the best yet.

Few have been as privileged as I have been to work with such an accomplished and supportive group of teacher educators—my Johnson State College colleagues past and present. I have also enjoyed my role as a regular guest speaker at Middlebury College teacher education seminars through the gracious invitation of its director, Gregg Humphrey.

My students over the years have taught me so much. I am proud to have been able to help prepare education students for their careers as elementary, middle, and high school teachers. Thank you, also, to all readers who have told me how useful *Positive Classroom Management* has been for you—I'm honored by your words.

In particular, I am obliged to a stellar role model whose spirit remains with me. Early in life, I had the special inspiration of a master teacher, my Aunt Flora Gigante. She was my godmother as well, and in our large extended family, she was its pride and joy. In my 5-year-old eyes and to all who knew her, Flora Gigante personified *una bella persona*: She was smart and stylish and seemed to stand 7 feet tall. One of the first Italian-American women to be appointed to a principalship of a New York City public school, Aunt Flora was my hero. Each summer she traveled the world, bringing objects, ideas, and stories to her students (and godson) from Asia, Africa, Central America, and every other conceivable point on the globe. She brought me books and dreams. Most of all, Aunt Flora aroused my interest in other cultures, enhancing my curiosity to experience it, to travel, to learn. Her enthusiasm for teaching others about this world was, literally, highly contagious.

A very practical woman, Aunt Flora would show me around her Bronx, New York, public school, introducing me—politely and importantly—to her teachers, all the time privately relating to me what each teacher did well. She was a most positive educator: capable, strong, and, when necessary, tough. But even when she was tough, my aunt was never severe or vindictive. She was *positively* tough. I never heard my aunt blame or complain. She never belittled students or teachers, nor did she ever act victimized. Instead of pointing a finger of blame, Aunt Flora pointed to models of excellence, made clear her expectations, then worked toward what she valued. Her inspiration drew me to teaching, and I have not once regretted that decision.

Corwin Press thanks the following reviewers for their contributions to this book:

Alan Canestrari
Assistant Professor of Education
Roger Williams University
Bristol, RI

Jill Lindberg
Supervisor, Milwaukee Public Schools Special
    Education Internship Program
University of Wisconsin
Milwaukee, WI

Marilyn L. Page
Technology Coordinator, Social Studies
    Teacher Education Programs
Pennsylvania State University
University Park, PA

Rita Schaerer King
International Educational Consultant
Murfreesboro, TN

About the Author

Robert C. Di Giulio is a professor and education researcher at Johnson State College in Vermont. He earned his PhD in human development from the University of Connecticut and his DEd in socio-education from the University of South Africa. He earned his BA and MS from St. John's University and Brooklyn College, respectively. Dr. Bob began his teaching career in the New York City public school system, where he taught for a number of years. His 35-year career as an educator includes teaching at the elementary, middle, junior high, and college levels, with experience ranging from crowded urban schools to a one-room schoolhouse. He has also served as an elementary school principal, educational consultant, speaker, and writer.

As an educational consultant, Dr. Bob codeveloped TeenTest, a vocational counseling program for adolescents. He also coauthored educational computer software called Language Activities Courseware and authored its teacher's guide. His *Teacher* magazine article "The 'Guaranteed' Behavior Improvement Plan" was recognized as having one of the highest total readership scores of any of the magazine's articles.

Dr. Bob has authored numerous books, including *When You Are a Single Parent*, *Effective Parenting*, *Beyond Widowhood*, and *Losing Someone Close*. His journal *After Loss* was selected by *Reader's Digest* as its featured condensed book in May 1994. He is a contributing author to *The Oxford Companion to Women's Writing in the United States* and *Marriage and Family in a Changing Society* and the coauthor of *Straight Talk About Death and Dying*. Most recently he has written *Great Teaching: What Matters Most in Helping Students Succeed* and coauthored *A Compass for the Classroom* with noted author Noah ben Shea.

His professional interests lie in teacher education, international education, teaching English as a foreign language (TEFL), and researching nonviolent classroom interventions. Recently Dr. Bob was named a

Fulbright Scholar, and he served as Fulbright Professor at the University of Jyväskylä in Finland, where he developed a new teacher education course and an interdisciplinary course called A Culture of Violence: U.S. and International Perspectives. In 2003 he served as a delegate to the United Nations Educational, Scientific, and Cultural Organization (UNESCO) Conference on Teaching and Learning for Intercultural Understanding. Dr. Bob resides with his family in northern Vermont.

Introduction

Teachers Are Our Last and Best Hope

The headlines almost scream at us: "Our schools are failing," "Our students do more poorly than students in other countries," "Teacher education needs revamping," "Parents give teachers little support." No day passes without our hearing or reading despairing words about the state of education and our schools. Despite their ominous tones and politically correct cynicism, there's really nothing new about these types of reports. They are timeless. The report of the New Hampshire public schools for the year 1853 (New Hampshire Board of Education) revealed a remarkably identical attitude: In 1853, too many students dropped out, and too few behaved well or gave much effort to their studies. The school day was fragmented, filled with too many subjects and too much "hurry and confusion" (p. 21). In 1853, teachers were said to be poorly trained, poorly paid, and overwhelmed by their duties. School boards held students and teachers most responsible for this state of affairs, yet they also roundly castigated parents for doing a poor job of child rearing, specifically in teaching good behavior and etiquette. Nothing new there!

Indeed, those blamed back in 1853—students, parents, and teachers—are the same ones who continue to be blamed for the state of our educational system (although today we have added a new culprit to the litany of the blamed: the schools themselves—those *failing schools*). But the truth remains that although hype and fear still work to sell soap and newspapers, blaming has not helped public education over the past 150 years.

Why?

Blaming prevents us from taking constructive action toward resolution of a problem.

This applies to all targets in the blame game: students, parents, teachers, and failing schools. Take, for example, how we blame students. It is especially odd for us educators to blame students. Even given the least capable of students, our business is to teach them, not judge them. Our job is to arouse curiosity, not condemn indifference. If a student truly cannot learn, then of what use can a teacher possibly be? If kids are born unteachable, how can teachers justify their jobs? (It is like the joke about the psychiatrist who dismissed his patient with the words, "I can't help you. You're crazy!")

Parents continue to be popular targets for censure. A Harris survey of more than 1,000 teachers revealed that 71% agreed that "lack of parental supervision at home" was a "major factor" contributing to school violence (Metropolitan Life Insurance Company, 1993, pp. 35–38). More recent surveys concur, indicating worry about young people's exposure to indecency and violence on TV and in music lyrics, video games, movies, and the Internet. Almost 80% of respondents to a Pew Research survey said parents were primarily to blame when children and adolescents are exposed to these media (Pew Research Center for the People & the Press, 2005). Yes, it is primarily the parents' job to raise their children, but blaming parents is just as fruitless as blaming students, for if students we see in school seem to be desperately lost and acting poorly, imagine how poorly their parents' lives are progressing. It is a waste of time to blame parents, and it is unrealistic to hope that the latest state and federal accountability measures directed at our so-called *failing schools* will improve the quality of school life for millions of children—or for their teachers. (Or, for that matter, for their parents or communities.)

Despite years of studies, commissions, blue-ribbon panels, and here-today-gone-tomorrow talk about school restructuring, public schools and their students—our young people—are still not a national priority, perhaps even less of one than they were in 1853. (Or in the year 2000. Does anyone remember the outcome of Goals 2000, the major American public school improvement initiative endorsed in 1991 and 1992 by 50 governors and two U.S. presidents from both major parties? Were any of the six goals for U.S. public schools met by the year 2000? Has any goal been met after the year 2000?)

Then who is most to blame? Students? Teachers? Failing schools? Bad karma? None of the above, because no matter how accurately it appears to be directed, blame still gets us nowhere. Blaming prevents us from taking constructive action toward resolution of a problem.

What works?

Taking charge of what we can change does work, and it works spectacularly.

As a new teacher, when I first heard feelings of desperation and cynicism expressed by my fifth- and sixth-grade inner-city students, I was taken aback. Like other middle-class teachers, I was surprised by their wrath and their view of the world as an evil, dangerous place. Like all child victims, they blamed themselves for their poverty and their disadvantaged lot in life.

Yes, their pain was real, but despite my frustration with a social and political system that I believed perpetuated this underclass, I felt strongly that answers—to their victimization, to their anger, to their antisocial behaviors—had to come from within each of us. Yes, we needed to continue speaking up for adequate funding and resources (and still need to do so today), but we also had to start changing the world right in our classrooms. Change would be local—starting small and letting it grow. I also realized that the burden of responsibility was on the teacher—me. As the only one in the classroom with even a modicum of power, I had to use it wisely, to provide leadership and an impetus for change. They desperately needed a model—something different from what they knew outside of school. Moreover, that model had to be real and tangible. Words alone were inadequate. I had to plan, work toward, and create a classroom environment that exemplified the type of world I spoke to them about. I had to back up my words with action. Although I never worked so hard in my life as I did my first 5 years in teaching, I quickly learned that taking charge of what could be changed got results. Several years later, when I held my first position as school principal and after 4 years of hard work by our entire school staff, our school (in one of the poorest towns in the state) was identified as a School With Exemplary Discipline by Phi Delta Kappa's Commission on Discipline at Ohio State University.

THE BAD NEWS AND THE GOOD NEWS

Our experience was far from unique. Most teachers who teach well and with a strong commitment to students describe their work modestly.

They typically do not see what they do as being highly unusual, having a simple but firm conviction that all students can do well, will do well, and that what the teacher does is pivotal to each student's success.

The bad news: It's work.

1. Done well, teaching is at times *a hard job*

All teachers know that teaching is labor-intensive—it can feel like a hard job at times. For instance, teaching demands we think on our feet (as well as think while we're off our feet, and even think while we're sleeping!). Teachers make more evaluation-related decisions than do members of any other occupation or profession, including physicians and stockbrokers. They must constantly be taking in information, processing it, and making decisions that are in the best interests of their students.

2. Done well, teaching is *time-intensive*

Besides being labor-intensive, teaching is time-intensive: The workload does not end at dismissal time! Indeed, teaching demands more time spent in preparation than any other profession or occupation does. The preparation is ongoing, and frankly, never-ending over the course of the year.

Done well, teaching is a rewarding but sometimes stressful job fraught with many challenges. National Education Association polls of teacher opinion typically show that addressing classroom discipline is American teachers' most pressing and most often mentioned challenge. The public is also concerned: In the annual Gallup Polls of the Public's Attitudes Toward the Public Schools, published each September in *Phi Delta Kappan*, discipline appears at or near the top of the list of most serious problems facing our schools.

And the good news: It's worth it

The hard work is worth it, because setting up and carrying out a positive classroom is both attainable and rewarding—rewarding for students, for teachers, for parents and community, and for our larger society.

What are some practical reasons why teachers (and future teachers) should aim to set up and maintain a positive classroom?

1. Academics: A positive classroom increases student learning and achievement.

The first and most basic reason is that student learning and achievement are at stake. Research clearly shows that students learn more—and more efficiently—in smooth-running classrooms. In an analysis of 50 years of educational research findings, of the 28 factors evaluated, classroom management had the greatest effect on student achievement (Wang, Haertel, & Walberg, 1993/1994). Later research confirmed that it is our teachers' actions in the classroom that matter most, having "twice the impact" of "school policies regarding curriculum, assessment, staff collegiality, and community involvement" (Marzano & Marzano, 2006, p. 24).

In addition to research, common sense tells us that a chaotic classroom distracts students, preventing them from attending, focusing, and concentrating. Disorder wastes time and hinders students from reaching their educational potential, and from developing their social and emotional intelligences. In a disruptive classroom environment, it is unlikely that children or adolescents can learn much about how to treat themselves and others respectfully.

2. Practicality: A positive classroom makes teaching easier. Or simply possible.

Second, a positive, smooth-running classroom makes a teacher's job easier, and it makes teaching possible, bringing a sense of accomplishment. Over the years that I have been engaged in teacher preparation, I have gotten to know many new students—some over 40 years of age—who have come to our teacher education program wanting to change careers and spend their working hours doing something fulfilling and valuable. Yes, except for the lousy pay, teaching can be among the most fulfilling and rewarding of professions. Having a positive classroom is the key to that fulfillment and reward: No teacher ever felt a sense of accomplishment while suffocated by an unruly, tumultuous classroom.

3. Quality: A positive classroom is reflective of teacher competency.

Third, your job and your career are at stake. Whether or not you think it's fair, your competence as a teacher will be judged largely by how well you set up and run that classroom. Indeed, difficulty with doing just that drives many teachers into other professions. Almost half of all New York City public school teachers either quit teaching entirely within their first 5 years on the job, or they leave to teach outside the New York City public school system (*Gotham Gazette*, 2003).

4. Responsibility: A positive classroom shows you're taking your legal duty of care seriously.

Fourth, you could be the defendant in a lawsuit. No teacher has yet been successfully sued for a student's failure to learn, yet teachers have been sued successfully when plaintiffs' lawyers convinced a judge or jury that a student's injury was due to teacher negligence. Of course, some student injuries are unforeseeable, and unforeseeable serious injury can happen in the best-run classrooms headed by experienced teachers. Nonetheless, teachers who create and maintain a safe and orderly environment for students—a positive classroom—will be in an advantageous position if they ever must defend themselves in court.

5. Utility: Society needs it desperately.

Finally, our society needs positive classrooms . . . desperately. A teacher's leadership and influence have never been more consequential. Although parents are still the number one influences on children's development (as they should be), schools are being asked to shoulder more responsibility than ever before. Whether we agree with it or not, this new responsibility has increasingly become part of each teacher's job. In a free society like ours, the stakes are high. Except for social workers and trial lawyers, today's teachers are the only professionals our society has—and will have in the future—to stand between a student and jail. If students fail to develop their social and emotional abilities and learn civil behavior, their misbehavior ultimately becomes a matter for the legal system and the corrections (prison) system.

Aggravating this predicament are the by-products of technology, and the change brought by technology itself. In the 1960s, media experts enthusiastically supposed that "electronic technology fosters and encourages unification and involvement" (McLuhan & Fiore, 1967, p. 8). They predicted that television and electronic media would re-create "the world in the image of a global village" (p. 67), bringing us closer together. But quite the opposite seems to have occurred: Besides providing practical and entertainment benefits, television and computers have also served to isolate us and insulate us from each other.

Because of increased television viewing at home, the likelihood that both parents work outside the home, and the decline of the influence of extended families and peer interactions, school is not only a good place for teaching and reinforcing students' positive behavior; it has now become, in many school districts both wealthy and poor, the best place students can learn empathic behavior.

Think about the simple act of eating together. In many American homes today, between the end of school and bedtime, it's only an adolescent, a microwave oven, and television. As a result, for millions of children and adolescents, school provides the main meal of the day, the only opportunity they have to eat with others, and thus a key opportunity for students to learn social skills. Yes, this redefines the role of school, but we already know that developing students' emotional literacy means "an expanded mission for schools," and in order for schools to take up their role in socializing children and adolescents, teachers must "go beyond their traditional mission," and community members must become increasingly involved with schools (Goleman, 1995, p. 279).

Researchers at the Harvard School of Public Health analyzed the results from 20 years of studies on child behavior (Buka & Earls, 1993), concluding that behavior problems in early childhood are the strongest predictors of violent and antisocial behavior later in life. In looking at teenage and adult subjects who as children participated in programs such as Head Start, one researcher reported that social skills learned in childhood are durable. EQ and empathy skills learned by children in Head Start stayed with them as adolescents, even if their academic gains eventually faded (Whitmire, 1994). There is little question that the time and effort teachers spend helping students develop emotional intelligence is an investment in the future, part of an expanded mission for our schools well worth having for its benefit to our society. The bottom line is worth repeating: Teachers may be our last, best, and only hope for addressing the more serious social issues that face our society: respecting human differences, honoring human dignity, and ensuring our survival as a people.

Setting up and running a positive classroom is within reach of all teachers. The techniques and skills can be learned. I believe that during the next 10 to 20 years those educators who successfully help students develop empathic behavior will become prized members of our local and national communities. (Who knows? Maybe we will also begin to pay teachers according to that contribution!)

PART I

The Positive Classroom

Toward a Positive Classroom

Moving Beyond Rules and Reactions

Before speaking about specific strategies that create a positive classroom, I want us to think about what we already know about students and classrooms. In its broadest sense, setting up and running a positive classroom means a great deal more than discipline, or making students behave. We know too much today about how people learn to fall back on old techniques that use compliance and fear to secure discipline. We know (but still try to ignore the fact) that humans develop at different rates. We know that children and adolescents possess a rich array of intelligences, each of which can be developed to an average or greater-than-average level of capability. We know that EQ (emotional intelligence) is more critical for success than IQ (intelligence quotient). We know rewards can feel like punishments, and vice versa. In short, we have learned more about child and adolescent development in the past 50 years than we have over the past 2,000 years. Furthermore, we've learned more about human learning in those same 50 years than we have in any previous human era. Given this new knowledge, the only real problem as I see it is not the lack of information but the forces that allow some of this knowledge while suppressing other aspects. For example, there is political will that holds standardized test scores to be valid indicators of what students know and don't know. Whether this is correct or not is a matter for debate, but what is clearly true is that assessments based on standardized tests are *least informative* for teachers, students, and parents, especially in light of what we know (or should know) today: Our students have rich cognitive and emotional intelligences, varied interests, and different levels of maturity, motivation, and needs. Standardized tests are simply unable to recognize or measure any of these.

Similarly, we have to be careful of the ways we assess our teachers. We must see that an effective classroom teacher is far more than a great test score coach, efficient manager, or strict disciplinarian. There is a lot more to do than manage and control, especially if we seek a classroom environment where the teacher gets things going, keeps things moving, keeps students safe, and runs the show well enough to actually teach and help students learn and grow. At its heart, setting up the positive classroom is creative: It creates the best situation in which the student can learn and the teacher can teach.

At their worst, classrooms can be negative and adversarial situations: Teacher is pitted against student, and students are pitted against one another and the teacher. However, the needs of the learner and those of the teacher are not naturally at odds. Teaching and learning need not be a zero-sum game; one side does not have to lose so that the other side can win. Yet when classrooms are negative and punitive, teacher action is replaced by teacher reaction and adversarial behavior. No amount of "managing" can save that situation.

Why does this happen? Why do teachers react as adversaries to students? Because teachers are human. Under stress, humans instinctively fear losing control. Faced with a highly stressful classroom situation, teachers find that their choices quickly get narrowed down to two: They can either cave in and be perceived as ineffectual, or they can dig in, come down hard, and resort to harsh, reactive methods to try to restore order.

A GET-TOUGH APPROACH

For some teachers, a new classroom is as fearsome as a cave filled with bats. Faced with the need to prepare, plan, carry out their plans, organize, prioritize, and evaluate, some teachers are overwhelmed. They simply do not know what to do or where to begin. In response to this confusion, teachers may adopt a get-tough approach. Such an approach, which attempts to subdue students with rules, threats, and punishments, cannot teach good behavior. Similarly, assertive classroom management packages rely heavily on punishment and other external controls—checks placed on a chalkboard or marbles in a jar. In such packaged plans, the teacher is promoting not heartfelt, empathic behavior but conformity to reactive, impersonal rules. Students may momentarily comply for fear of punishment, yet the good behavior these plans produce is short-lived. Because good behavior has not been internalized, it cannot carry over to other settings such as the school yard or lunchroom. Worst of all, these plans can turn a teacher into a dizzy robot whose time and attention are focused more on detecting and apprehending culprits than on teaching.

A LAISSEZ-FAIRE APPROACH

At the other extreme is a laissez-faire classroom approach, which provides students with no structure or guidance and may be just as detrimental to student dignity as overregulation. Anyone can give kids freedom by letting them to do whatever pleases them. Remember that all students need to feel safe in school if they are to learn, and that safety includes protection from being harmed or ridiculed by other students. All students need freedom of choice and to experience empowerment—to have a say in what they are learning—in the context of a secure, democratic learning environment. Consequently, classrooms must be positive: They must promote students' healthy social and emotional development in a safe environment. Ultimately, our schools must teach students how to get their needs met without resorting to deceit or violence to themselves or others. That's a big, important job.

MANAGING A BUSINESS VERSUS MANAGING A CLASSROOM

Some are wary of the idea of *management*, thinking it implies unfair power manipulation. Because we hear all too often how power is wielded by government and business leaders, teachers may be uncomfortable using their power to run a classroom. What I am suggesting is that teachers need to use their power, but in a way different from the way it is used in business.

Compare business to teaching: In business, the goal is making a profit, while the goal of schooling is not profit but the education of students. To achieve their goals, businesses use rewards—salary, bonuses, commissions—and punishments—pay cuts, demotion, and, ultimately, firing of those who do not measure up or are expendable. Whereas employees who have been fired simply move on to find work elsewhere, students cannot pick up and leave so easily. Students who are fired must stay, relegated to an existence as losers or failures. These labels stick, residing within the student's self-concept long after the student has dropped out or finished school.

Although some school reformers have suggested that schools should be run like businesses, the problem, coincidentally, is just that: For the most part, schools *are* run like businesses. Each day countless well-meaning teachers use the same reward and punishment techniques as the ones used in business, and they wind up firing students through suspension and expulsion. The number of fired students is not trivial: In 2000, over 3 *million* U.S. students were suspended and/or expelled from public elementary and secondary schools (United States Department of Education, 2004), the majority of them for nonviolent, non-drug-related offenses, namely, truancy and tardiness (Center on Juvenile and Criminal Justice, 2002).

To summarize, whereas the bottom line of a corporation is profit for the benefit of that corporation and its shareholders, the bottom line of a school is the education of students for the benefit of both the individual student and the larger society. Hence, schools' methods toward achieving those goals must be constructive and inclusive, not punitive and exclusionary. Failed businesses end up in a bankruptcy court's file cabinet, but educationally and socially bankrupt students do not so simply and effortlessly disappear.

THE DAMAGING EFFECTS OF REACTIVE RULES

Fortunately, there are alternatives to shaping our schools along the lines of businesses, and there are also alternatives to using reward-and-punishment, reactive rules in the classroom. Think about this: Human civilizations that have survived longest are those with no formal crime-and-punishment systems. The Netsilik Eskimos of northern Canada, for example, have thrived under inhospitable conditions for 10,000 years without formal laws. They have long valued what we call today emotional intelligence, having realized EQ is essential for survival. The essence of Netsilik EQ emanates from three central, unwritten codes of conduct: *collaboration*, where all work together in hunting, preparing, and sharing food; *kinship*, the maintenance of a network of ties to nuclear and extended family; and *patterned relationships*, the forming of partnerships (dyads) that bring unrelated people together in an almost impossibly hostile Arctic world (Balikci, 1970, chaps. 3–6). Behavior beneficial to the society is taught personally, through codes of conduct. To enforce these codes, Netsilik rely not on courts or prisons, but on social pressure. Membership in society is valued; thus, the desire to avoid being ostracized is a potent force. Without having to label its members as either law-abiding or criminals, Netsilik society promotes behavior that is productive both to the individual and to the Netsilik as a whole. In short, Netsilik EQ keeps people safe, healthy, and connected to each other. In fancier terms, it is a reciprocal and empathic survival system.

Because our larger society is so complex and impersonal, it cannot use person-to-person, Netsilik-type understandings (handshakes don't seal agreements any longer!). Instead, our society must rely on an impersonal and formalized law system of police, lawyers, courts, and prisons, and even these measures are of questionable effectiveness. Between 1993 and 2003, levels of the most serious violent crimes (rape, robbery, aggravated assault, and homicide) did decline, but drug cases and felony convictions increased (United States Department of Justice, 2005c). Still, U.S. rates of violent crime remain high compared to those of other industrialized nations. Plus, expenditure "for each of the major criminal justice functions (police, corrections, judicial) has been increasing" (United States Department of Justice, 2005a). So it remains doubtful that traditional criminal justice responses prevent violence, even with great financial expenditure for those responses. Even the idea that incarceration works to lower the crime rate by simply keeping a prisoner locked up is flawed. Yes, today there are more prisoners than ever before, but even with the numbers being high, the average prison sentences being longer than ever, and there being a relatively low number of new offenders, given the likelihood that the traditionally high level of recidivism will remain high as prisoners are released, the total criminality numbers are staggering—higher by far than at any time in our past, and worrisome indeed.

Laws and reactive rules may be a necessary evil of the real world, but they are inappropriate in the smaller world of a classroom of teachers and students. The classroom works best when it works as a person-to-person, small, and simple society, like that of the Netsilik Eskimos. Unfortunately, many teachers assume that because reactive rules and laws are part of our larger world, they must also comprise the heart of a classroom.

When teachers use this impersonal larger-society approach to their teaching, they set up ways to identify and punish criminality but rarely get down to actually teaching good behavior. However, because classrooms are not huge and complex societies, we teachers can take a small-society approach to classroom management.

Of course, today's classrooms are diverse in ways that Netsilik society is not. We teach students from different ethnic and racial groups, and from families with very different values. Nevertheless, these differences highlight the necessity for teachers to focus on helping students realize what they have in common: As human beings, we all need to feel safe, to survive, to love and be loved, to be accepted as part of a group, and to grow in wisdom and self-knowledge. This is true for every human being irrespective of class, race, gender, ethnic group, or other classification. It is true for high school students and kindergartners alike.

The positive classroom is a place where teachers establish basic understandings through person-to-person interaction, where all can discuss and agree upon limits and practice adhering to them, and ultimately model and learn empathic behavior. The positive classroom works well for developing students' EQ, too. To move toward the creation of that positive setting, we must first distinguish rules that teach (proactive rules) from rules that do not (reactive rules).

Perhaps the biggest drawback to reactive rules is that when they work, they work only after the fact. Although they may threaten punishment, they do not *prevent* misbehavior. Using reactive rules, we create a ticking time bomb, waiting for an infraction to occur so we can impose consequences. Until there is an actual infraction, reactive rules are powerless and, in effect, teach nothing (except perhaps a vague sense of fear). Yes, our justice system relies on reactive rules, but it does not follow that our classrooms should also be built on them. We can't wait for something to go wrong before dealing with it, and we can't hold students on the tenterhooks of fear, waiting for something bad to happen!

Indeed, reactive rules and laws create more problems than they solve. The United States has more laws than the rest of the world combined, and its government makes use of those laws: The United States has a higher percentage of its population in prison than any other industrialized nation. By 2005, 2.1 million Americans were in prison (United States Department of Justice, 2005b). Nearly 7 million Americans were on probation, in jail, in prison, or on parole; thus 3.2% of all adult residents of the United States, or 1 out of every 31 U.S. adults, is within the correctional system. That system keeps getting more efficient: Over the past 10 years, the number of prisoners has increased annually. Yes, our law system efficiently identifies criminals, but in doing so it creates another problem: what to do with them. Once we have called people criminals, the only thing we can do is build prisons to hold them. As the number of criminals grows, so must the number of prisons. This is an expensive, stopgap arrangement for society, but within our schools, reactive rules provide no recourse. What can schools do with students who are the school's identified criminals? Schools can only put them out—suspend them and expel them. Ultimately, the more students we suspend and expel, the fewer schools we will need, but the fewer schools we have, the more prisons we will need. Researchers Skiba and Peterson (1999) point out, "In choosing control and exclusion as our preferred methods of dealing with school disruption, even as we refrain from positive interventions, we increase the likelihood that the correctional system will become the primary agency responsible for troubled youths" (p. 381).

The growing similarity between large schools and prisons is striking. Crimes—particularly serious violent crimes—are much more likely to occur in larger U.S. schools. Large schools (1,000 or more students) have more than three times more violent crime than small and medium-sized schools (United States Department of Education, 1998). The value of smaller schools continues to be affirmed in later research (Wasley, 2002).

Permit me to highlight three types of rules that are highly damaging, undermining emotional intelligence and working against the positive classroom. Then I will discuss a fourth type: Proactive rules that teach and that help our students grow in empathic, positive behavior.

REACTIVE RULES, TYPE I: RULES THAT THREATEN

My analogy between prisons and schools is not abstract or far-fetched. A few years ago, 30 girls at a Connecticut middle school were strip-searched by a gym teacher, assistant principal, and security guard after a student claimed that $50 was missing. Threatened with arrest if they refused to take off their clothing, all 30 girls complied. No money was found. In response to students' and parents' outrage, the school superintendent suspended the three women who conducted the strip-search, and he apologized to the girls and their families (Schuster, 1997). Four years later, New York City settled a separate $50 million class-action strip-search lawsuit (Sebok, 2001).

There are educators who support strong responses (like strip-searches), thinking them appropriate to crimes (like theft) that are suspected to have occurred. However, there is no evidence that these responses in any way reduce school crime or violence (Skiba & Peterson, 1999), and there is evidence that strip searches may create emotional harm in students (Hyman & Perone, 1998). Yes, fear works: Children and adolescents—all humans—do respond to threats of physical punishment (or arrest), and will comply to avoid harm. But because people comply does not mean that they have internalized the right values. They may simply have learned how not to get caught next time.

We still hear "let the punishment fit the crime." But besides the fact that punishments fail to teach people what *to* do, there is another downside: Punishments can actually *exempt* students from learning empathic behavior. Conventional wisdom tells us that punishment (or at least the threat of it) is a necessity in teaching students good behavior, but think about it: Punishment or the threat of punishment actually sabotages the process. Punishment relieves the student from an obligation to behave with empathy, or, in other words, to act with consideration for the well-being of others. With rules that threaten, students have this choice: "Don't break the rule, or break it and take the punishment." Students can thus trade their willingness to suffer punishment for their duty to respect one another. The real drawback is that when rules that threaten do not work (which is usually the case), the only thing a teacher can do is raise the stakes by making the punishment increasingly distasteful in the hope that fewer will opt for it. Yet this can lead down a dark and twisted path for those who will accept increasingly strong punishment in order to avail themselves of their choice to hurt another. Certainly, we can (and should) provide our students with many choices during the school day, but showing empathy—honoring the basic humanity of others—must not be negotiable, because its flip side, in extreme cases, is sociopathic behavior and violence.

REACTIVE RULES, TYPE II: RULES THAT MISLEAD

Rules mislead us when we think it is the words that teach, instead of the real human social interaction that the words describe. Humans—children, adolescents, adults—do not learn the positive—how *to* behave—from rules. Cognitive development giants Piaget and Vygotsky tell us that written and verbal rules and laws are too abstract for young children (they take rules literally and keep them external to their thinking). Rules are also external to older children and preteens, who internalize them only as their social relationships develop, modifying them to the circumstances at hand (Reimer, Paolitto, & Hersh, 1983, pp. 39–42).

Rules mislead and do not teach when they are expressed in the negative. For example, it's one thing to have a school rule "No swearing allowed," but it is another matter to teach students how to express themselves constructively and then actually expect them to speak to each other without using vulgarity. It's one thing to say "No bullying," but it is an entirely better strategy to teach students how to treat each other respectfully—an ongoing lesson as appropriate for high schoolers as it is for kindergartners.

Rules that mislead can also give a teacher a false sense of security. A classroom I visited as a principal provides an illustration. Picture this: Above the chalkboard was a computer-generated banner almost the width of the classroom. It was a list of 10 rules, printed in huge boldface uppercase letters. The teacher was puzzled when, by October 1, her class was out of control. She had clearly posted the rules, and she told me she had even involved her students in coming up with the list.

What was wrong with that picture?

One thing. As I sat to discuss the situation with the teacher, she realized she had never gotten around to actually *teaching her students* the expected behaviors; she had simply taught what the rules were and expected that to be sufficient. There had been no follow-up, no putting the words into practice, only one huge banner. She had assumed that rules spoke for themselves. "After all," she said, "I made the rules clear. I posted them in big letters, too!"

REACTIVE RULES, TYPE III: RULES THAT DISTORT

Finally, there are rules that keep students from being accountable for their behavior. Rules that distort can lead to warped perceptions on the part of the students. Particularly when expressed legally or formally, such rules can foster a distorted sense of justice by transforming a clever student into a classroom lawyer, engaging the teacher in arguments over the precise interpretation of classroom or school rules. Some adolescents are particularly adept at this. Although debating may sharpen a student's argumentation skills, it serves to divert focus from the point of the rule in the first place. Worse, students can develop a distorted idea of justice: "If I argue successfully, then no rule has been broken, and because no rule was broken, I did nothing wrong!" We read of public figures, accused of a crime, flatly denying wrongdoing. In our innocent-until-proven-guilty tradition, every accused is always accurate in proclaiming his or her innocence! By arguing skillfully, many who have behaved wrongly are found not guilty.

With a rule like "Keep your hands to yourselves," punching another is wrong *even if there are no witnesses.* Punching another is wrong, even if you can produce witnesses who say that she first swore at you. Punching another is wrong, even if there is no rule that states, "No punching." So if I ask you if you punched her, I need you to be truthful: "I will take what you tell me as truth, and want you to know that as your teacher, I will be truthful with you as well."

Hence, learning empathic behavior demands that teachers shift students' focus away from arguing *why* they did something (the accused's side of a story) to considering *what* their action did to another. Learning empathic behavior means that we (students and teachers) will be truthful with each other, even if it means that I may disapprove of what you did, or hold you to make amends to Jessica.

Ultimately, reactive rules are signs of desperation. In our classrooms, bigger and more menacing punishments cannot teach students to care about others or think about their own behavior.

PROACTIVE RULES: RULES THAT TEACH

Before you think I'm advocating anarchy in the classroom, let me restate: Successful teachers establish limits and recognize natural consequences, yet they do not depend on rules and punishments to do their teaching. Experienced, successful teachers (including my sample of outstanding teachers) avoid impersonal, crime-and-punishment classroom management. Instead, they set up a classroom community. They use expectations for behavior before the fact. One high school teacher told me, "Each school year begins with an in-depth discussion of the term 'respect' and all that it entails in our classroom." Another wrote, "We spend a lot of time in class talking about, demonstrating, and highlighting appropriate behavior." A third teacher advised, "Model respectful, caring behavior for your students and directly teach the skills—don't assume or leave it to chance." But what attitudes, knowledge, and skills do successful teachers actually teach? What is their alternative to relying on reactive rules? The answer is that they involve their students in creating the rules by providing an opportunity for them to think about, discuss, and put into action positive expectations for human behavior. The rules that are created in this way are powerful and empowering, for they are proactive instead of reactive. They are what I call *basic understandings*, essential to the life of every classroom, kindergarten through college. The next chapter is devoted to these all-important *rules that teach*.

Creating Basic Understandings

Ways We Can Grow (and Survive) Together

Almost 100 years ago, French sociologist Emile Durkheim said that in order for young people to learn empathic behavior (which values the welfare of others as well as self), they must first be oriented toward the well-being of others, or what he called *collectivity*. "Moral behavior," he wrote, "demands an inclination toward collectivity" (Durkheim, 1925/1961, p. 233). Before we can hope that students will learn *how* to behave well, we must first ensure that they possess *a desire* (inclination) to behave well. Durkheim emphasized that this inclination does not happen automatically. It must be taught, and here is where schools come in: While family and home are essential to socialization, Durkheim felt that teachers and schools are in an even better position to teach moral behaviors. He pointed out that it's quite natural for us to love our parents and siblings, but learning how to get along with strangers is a behavior that is not inborn, although it forms the foundation of society where we interact with those to whom we are not related.

Today, Howard Gardner (1983, 1993) and Daniel Goleman (1995) have addressed intelligences that underlie development of those moral behaviors to which Durkheim referred. Gardner speaks of *interpersonal* and *intrapersonal* intelligences, and Goleman speaks of *emotional intelligence*, or EQ. Looking specifically at the role of schools in developing these intelligences, Goleman cites the 1978 work of Karen Stone and Harold Dillehunt, who identify "main components" of "The Self Science Curriculum" that address students' intelligences. These components (Goleman, 1995, pp. 303–304) include self-awareness, personal decision making, managing feelings, handling stress, empathy, communications, self-disclosure, insight, self-acceptance, personal responsibility, assertiveness, group dynamics, and conflict resolution. (These components are also descriptors of Howard Gardner's intrapersonal and interpersonal multiple intelligences.)

In creating the positive classroom, we use these types of components to work with our students in creating basic understandings. Already in place are basic *limits* (like those of personal space and personal property), which are the starting points for ongoing discussion and creation (and renewal) of basic understandings. Basic limits are those that students already possess or can easily comprehend. For example, "One person per seat" is a basic limit that needs no elaboration once mentioned by the teacher and is useful as a starting point in building basic understandings about personal space. This teacher-student work in creating basic understandings not only builds on basic limits, but also extends them. This is precisely the process that helps students develop their individual EQ (their emotional, interpersonal, and intrapersonal intelligences). This is fostered through *interaction*—with the teacher, with classmates, and with others in the school community. Concentrating on discussion and active listening, teachers can help students grow by revising and updating their existing conceptions of, for example, empathic behavior. Remember that our students (and all of us, in fact) are moral developers; we are constantly revising our sense of right and wrong based on our ongoing life experiences.

Here is an example of a fourth-grade discussion that helps create basic understandings. Note how the discussion incorporates at the same time two components (empathy and managing feelings) from The Self Science Curriculum:

"Last year Mrs. Marsh said we could bring water guns to class. I brought mine!"

"Did being able to bring a water gun make students happy, Graidy?"

"Yeah! When you got somebody good!" (All laugh.)

"But what about the kid who gets hit? Jacob, did you ever get squirted?"

"Yeah! In the back of Mrs. Marsh's class, three kids ganged up on me all at once! Tyler got me right in the face . . ."

"Did you think it was fun?"

"Well, sorta. No, I guess it was . . . embarrassing?"

"Alex?"

"I shot at my brother, but then he got so mad he spit in my face, and then I got mad so I punched him."

"Sophie?"

"Jacob got moved at lunch yesterday. Everyone kept laughing at him after he got squirted right in his ear . . ."

Note the process. Note the basic understandings being established:

1. Being a target isn't fun.

2. Humiliation is painful.

3. It makes us want to strike back.

Also note how rich this is, how it can incline students toward the good of others, and yet how different it is from a teacher's making and posting of "Do this or else" reactive rules.

What is perhaps most powerful about creating basic understandings is that teachers do not have to go through this process with every single item or issue. Students can—and will—generalize (extend) the basic understandings that are established. By extending them, students can apply them to other situations. If it is understood that being a target is not fun, students can apply this concept to other areas, such as group teasing, picking on a student, or ridiculing someone in front of others.

Take the second basic understanding: Humiliation is painful. Toys are fun to play with, but they can also be used to hurt others. In this case, when used to shoot water in peoples' faces, water guns have no real purpose other than humiliation. Thus, don't bring them to school. (Generalization: Other toys are best left home, too.) Perhaps a most relevant extension students can see is one especially important under-standing, given the urgent situation in too many contemporary schools:

Humiliation = pain = no water guns = no guns

Reactive rules, metal detectors, threats, security guards, and police dogs can never teach that basic understanding as effectively as can a simple but powerful discussion followed up by ongoing support for these basic understandings.

MORE BASIC UNDERSTANDINGS: A POSITIVE PRESCRIPTION

Before the school year begins, come up with a starter set of basic understandings (three or four) you believe are important to address with your students at the very beginning. (It's important that these resonate within yourself first, or else they remain somebody else's dictates.) Then, consulting a list of components like those comprising The Self Science Curriculum, decide which EQ components will be represented within each of these basic understandings. One caution bears mentioning at this point: *Be sure you're not in reality setting out a list of nonnegotiable reactive rules.* The basic understandings you select should be flexible, not in the sense that students can set moral behavior on its head ("Hitting people is okay"), but in the sense that everything is up for discussion. We must trust our students as human beings; we must trust that through their intelligence(s) and empathy and with our leadership (but not domination), they will be able to construct basic understandings that they and we can live with, even if the wording varies from our original design.

As an example, below is a starter list of four basic understandings I developed and used with my eighth-grade students. Lists like these— appropriate for elementary, middle school, or high school—should form the opening core of discussion, and can serve as a guide for you. During the course of the school year, more basic understandings can and should be created and practiced. (Basic understandings can also be very valuable to develop on a schoolwide basis with other teachers and students.)

Starter list of basic understandings:

1. Respect is nonnegotiable.
2. Cooperation over competition.
3. Achievement is valued.
4. Full inclusion applies.

---

1. *Respect is nonnegotiable.* All people need to be respected, and all students are people; they need to be respected by each other and by the teacher, and the teacher needs to be respected by them. This creates a foundation for all other basic understandings. For example, insulting others is to be avoided because insults damage human dignity.

Here is an example of a positive discussion around respect in a third-grade classroom:

"My mom's boyfriend Roy uses really bad words. 'Specially when he's mad."

"Yeah. I know what you mean. My brother is, like, always saying bad words."

"Kaitlin, how do you feel about it when it happens?"

"Terrible! I tell him to shut up, and so does Mom!"

"Wow. I can't tell my Uncle Roy to shut up, so I just walk into the other room."

"How can we be sure things are different in our classroom? Jamal?"

"We can't walk away, can we? We gotta stay in this room, don't we?"

"Emma?"

"We don't have to walk away if everybody treats everybody right. Have everybody be nice to each other. To say bad words only when they are by themselves, or outside, or when nobody can hear . . ."

"And we can just talk to each other when we're mad, and say 'I'm not happy with something' instead of saying bad words behind somebody's back."

"What about 'Shut up'? Jamal?"

"We can't say 'Shut up'—that's rude. Nobody should say it if everybody talks nice to each other."

"Yeah. If you're mad, you can just walk to someplace else in the classroom and not say anything. My dad says, 'If you don't have anything good to say, then just walk away.' You don't have to say 'Shut up' or anything. Just walk away."

Note the process. Note the basic understandings being established. (EQ components: *self-awareness, conflict resolution, handling stress.*) These basic understandings can be listed on poster board and displayed in a prominent place in the classroom as reminders for future reference:

A. Use words. Talk to each other.

B. If angry, wait until you can use kind words.

C. Separation is better than conflict.

2. *Cooperation over competition.* Most of the time, one student's helping another student solve a classroom science problem is not cheating or unfair. Our job is to help students clarify the difference. The best way to do so is to establish cooperation as a classroom norm. Specifically, this means planning and carrying out cooperative learning practices in the classroom by having students work in pairs and in small groups for at least half their time in school (see Slavin, 1994). From the basic understanding that cooperation is the norm, students can then learn that certain unusual situations (such as quiz- or test-taking) are competitive times, rare instances when cooperatively sharing information with another is not the right thing to do. Cooperative learning has another huge strength: Of all curricular, instructional, and assessment practices connected with teaching students with disabilities, cooperative learning is the most valuable strategy we can use to support inclusive education (National Center on Educational Restructuring and Inclusion, 1995; Villa & Thousand, 2006).

Here is an example of a positive discussion around cooperation in a middle-grades classroom:

"What is the difference between helping and cheating?"

"Well, cheating is when you get caught!"

"So if you don't get caught, Isabella, it's okay to cheat?"

"No . . . I'm not sure, actually."

"Cameron, you look like you're eager to speak. Go ahead."

"Cheating is when you think you are helping somebody, but you really are hurting them."

" 'Hurting them'? How do you mean that?"

"Well, if the teacher thinks it's Caleb's work, but it really isn't, it's like you're lying."

"When else do you not help someone? Andrew?"

"Um, if it's a test. You're not supposed to help somebody do their test."

"Yes. But what if you're both working together on a project? Is it okay to share answers?"

"Uh-huh! If Caleb is working with me on a science project, that's not cheating. We're helping each other learn—I have these great ideas, and he has neat handwriting. We make a good team!"

Again note the process, and note the basic understandings being established by this discussion. (EQ components: *personal responsibility, empathy, personal decision making.*)

A. Helping others is a normal thing to do.

B. Sometimes we work without helping others.

C. It's good to help and be helped.

3. *Achievement is valued.* Just as we need to set cooperation as the norm, we need to expect and welcome student achievement. One way we can do this is by broadening our view of what achievement is. Because schools traditionally emphasize language and math over other areas, many teachers use Howard Gardner's description of multiple intelligences (1983) as a guide to recognizing and teaching to musical, bodily-kinesthetic, spatial, naturalist, and other such intelligences. High school teachers have used Gardner's theory in many different content areas, which increases opportunities for older students to be successful. Most fundamental is a positive class attitude that values achievement, regardless of the areas of achievement themselves.

Here is an example of a positive discussion around achievement in a ninth-grade classroom:

"We have our four group winter performances coming up soon. It's going to be important to use all the talents you have in your group. Spend five minutes talking about the different jobs and roles we've listed on this chart, and talk about who in your group might do which jobs and roles."

"Stefan? What did your group come up with?"

"Well, Maria likes to talk—right?—so we thought she'd be a good narrator. Nathaniel can bring in his guitar and do music. I'm not good at anything, so . . ."

"Nothing? Let me ask Stefan's group. What does Stefan do well? Nathaniel?"

"Stefan can write the script out. He always gets great marks in English. His writing analysis assignments are usually the best in our class."

Once again note the process, and note the basic understandings being established by this discussion. (EQ components: *group dynamics, managing feelings, insight.*)

A. Different talents are important here.

B. Each of us excels at something.

C. We all value excellence.

4. *Full inclusion applies.* In a legal sense, *inclusion* means that under the law, a student must have equal access to educational materials and facilities. In the more important basic understanding sense, it means that a classroom is more than a collection of individuals. Inclusion in this sense means that students see and are inclined toward a common good—to consider the good of others in addition to their own individual good. They learn how to live with one another and how to be part of a group. Students learn how to get their needs met, but through their developing emotional intelligence and not by stepping on others. Hence inclusion sets the foundation for the small society of the classroom. (Remember the Netsilik?) All students belong here, and only under unusual circumstances are they absent from the classroom.

Here is an example of a positive discussion around inclusion in a fifth-grade classroom:

"In the school I used to go to, the kids were all stuck up. If you didn't have the right clothes, you were nobody."

"That sounds pretty bad to me, Latricia. Is it different here?"

"Yeah, well, a little. Actually it's mostly the same in this school, but I think it's different here in this class, if you know what I mean."

"Tell us more, Latricia."

"The kids here are my friends, and they care about each other. If they have a problem, instead of arguing they talk things out. That never used to happen in Mr. Martin's class last year."

"Sounds like you feel comfortable in our class. Great. Does anyone feel uncomfortable? Ethan?"

"No, I agree with Latricia. The kids here are like other kids—they're rude outside. But when we're here we're not jerks to each other."

"Why is that?"

"Maybe . . . maybe because we have to get along being all in the same room? Or maybe because we know each other better than we know the other kids. I'm not sure, but Latricia's right—it's a lot easier to get along in here than outside!"

"What do you say about this? Stefan?"

"I think it's really important to speak up for yourself. You can't just let things happen, and then feel bad at somebody over something. Last year in Mr. Martin's class we never had a chance to talk like this."

Again, note the process, and note the basic understandings being established by this discussion. (EQ components: *assertiveness, conflict resolution, self-disclosure*.)

A. This classroom (school) is a good place to be.

B. All of us can get our needs met.

C. Everyone here belongs here.

SUPPORTING THE BASIC UNDERSTANDINGS

No matter which components you choose to focus on, there are several essential classroom conditions that must exist for the basic understandings to take life and become real to your students and yourself. Here are six conditions that apply to a positive classroom at any grade level:

Safety: The classroom is a safe place

First, as evidenced by the sample discussions above, your classroom should be a safe place—a place for students to get their needs met. Students must feel free to speak and act without being ridiculed or ignored, and students need to be different without being excluded. In this, students will take their cues from the teacher; how you react to students' opinions and actions will be a powerful model for your students. You will also have to be the one to initiate the discussions and create a time during the day when they can take place.

Uniqueness: The classroom has a unique identity as a special place to be

Second, we all agree that "It takes an entire village to raise a child," and that the "classroom-as-village" is an ideal model of the larger community we all occupy outside of school—whether it be a future work environment, a social club or religious group, or a family circle, each of which is a village. No matter what the grade level of your students, your classroom must develop its unique identity as a special place to be. Draw in and use the resources at your disposal to create that village within your classroom. Sergiovanni (1994) says that schools must emphasize the creation of elementary and secondary classrooms that "resemble small family groups" (pp. 127–128). He explains that the key to stopping violence is to restore "a community of mind" among students. Without it, young people substitute for this loss in violent, antisocial ways. The recent movement toward creating houses—smaller units within larger middle and high schools—is an example of a way to move toward the concept of a village, but your classroom must be the smallest unit of all, and be unique in itself. This uniqueness can be easily created through symbolic identification—for example, having students' works displayed within the classroom—and through attributions that describe what is true and special about this group of students. This uniqueness can also arise from empowering students to serve as tutors or teachers of others within the classroom or school and make decisions that will really affect what students' activities include.

This is all nice and well, but there are things to look out for. To say it without attempting to overstate matters, we teachers need to be alert for harmful dynamics. Are cliques forming? Are pairs or groups of students acquiring a negative identity, acting like outcasts or losers? Is there bullying going on? If so, that will kill all of your attempts to empower students. In *Helping Students Fix Problems and Avoid Crises*, an excellent resource for teachers, Lawrence J. Greene warns that although students "possess the potential to be kind, . . . if left unchecked, a propensity for cruelty can become standard operating procedure. Unless this conduct is vigorously, consistently, and effectively discouraged, the malevolence could become an ingrained habit" (2005, p. 123). As a school principal, I have seen classes go from a Mr. Jones in June to a Ms. Smith in September—the exact same group of students—and undergo a remarkable transformation: On day one in September, Ms. Smith began vigorously, consistently, and effectively discouraging crude and bullying behavior. Putting aside the texts and tests for a few days, she spent class time openly sharing her concerns and helping students openly air their concerns, not focusing on bashing Mr. Jones but describing what they experienced as students in his classroom. This generated wonderful class discussions (and basic understandings) with students who only a few months earlier had been called "hopeless animals" by Mr. Jones. The good news is that Mr. Jones soon left teaching to make more money as a computer technician, and his former students were magically transformed from animals in a classroom jungle to good friends in a positive classroom. The even better news is that Ms. Smith is still teaching. True story.

Although their involvement fades in the upper grades, your students' parents are a key part of both their larger neighborhood community and your in-school, classroom community. Talk with them, send home stuff, and ask students to share with their parents the basic understandings you are working to establish. Don't compel parents to practice at home with their children or ask them to incorporate what you're doing into their private lives. That might be either insulting or an impossible task for some parents. You can best include parents by simply sharing with them what you are working toward, and let them take the ball from there.

Empathy: Empathic behavior is actively modeled and demonstrated to students

Third, empathic behavior is actively modeled and demonstrated to students. Don't be subtle about it, either. At a teachable moment, openly point out what you're trying to model. Students imitate what we do more than what we say, particularly when it comes to behavior. Point out how you are working with the other teachers for the annual junior class trip, or how several classes are cooperatively planning their Senior Day. Within your classroom, show sympathy when a student is hurt. (I am always amazed at how a teacher can use an injured kid as a teachable moment: "Well, maybe you were asking for it," they say, along with similar unhelpful taunts that make the hurt worse—and other students will emulate this attitude.)

In a fascinating study of the effects of adult modeling, researchers Bryan & Walbek (1970) had adults play a game with children in which the children could win money. Nearby was a box for donations to "poor children." Each adult sat and played a game with a child. The adult also pointed out the donation box, either complaining about it or advocating donating to it. Half the adults who advocated donating actually got up and donated, and half the adults who complained about donating actually donated as well. The outcome? Children tended to follow adults' *actions* rather than *words*: Those who saw an adult donate tended to do the same, *whether or not the adult spoke for or against donation*, and children who saw an adult not donate did not themselves donate, *even if the adult spoke in favor of donating.*

Rewards? Kept at a minimum

Fourth, in developing basic understandings, be cautious with rewards. Preferably, keep them at a minimum—especially material rewards. Although stickers, stars, and prizes can provide momentary fun, they send students the wrong message: "Behave in this way so that you will get a reward." Rewards lead people away from themselves, obliterating messages people have within themselves. Yes, we can and should praise behavior that is helpful to others and use it as a model: "Nick, you did a great job working as a team with Kaitlin and Madison today." "Emily, thank you for holding the door for Gabrielle—she had an armful of books!" "Sophia, I think it's splendid how you're helping Sarah get used to our class." But by materially rewarding students for simply cooperating, for respecting others, or for taking good care of their own bodies, we are introducing a distortion that clouds up what's inside each of us. A renowned opponent of using rewards as motivators, Alfie Kohn, the author of *Punished by Rewards* (1995), points out the futility of rewards when it comes to promoting fundamental and/or lasting growth within our students. Earlier, Kohn wrote that rewards "do not alter the attitudes that underlie our behaviors. They do not create an enduring commitment to a set of values or to learning; they merely, and temporarily, change what we do" (1993b, p. 784).

Realness: Basic understandings are established at a personal level

Fifth, don't hesitate to make things real. Don't be hesitant to establish basic understandings at a personal level. Basic understandings cannot work as abstract principles or formal rules the students subscribe to or promise to uphold. Words are all-too-easy ways we can deceive ourselves by confusing abstractions with reality—thinking, for example, that our students have actually learned good behavior whereas they have simply learned the talk and not the walk. In an early and often-cited study about cheating behaviors, students who cheated were just as likely to say that cheating was wrong as students who did not cheat at all (Hartshorne & May, 1930).

Yes, we want our students to take it personally, in the sense that each student is personally responsible for his or her actions. Class discussions must be geared not toward the production of rote repetition of platitudes but toward actual outcomes of personal action. Establishing basic understandings needs lots of pronouns—*I, our, me,* and *you*—and lots of verbs—*explained, helped, carried, read, showed,* etc.—but only a few adjectives—*cool, dumb, awesome, stupid* and so on: "Tell me about someone who helped out this morning. What did they do that was helpful?" Or, "I was pleased with how Cameron explained logging on to Tanya during computer class!" Or, "On Monday, we'll be getting a new student. His name is Muhammad, and he's a refugee from Sudan. What are some things we can do to help Muhammad feel welcome?"

Innovation: New and creative methods address old and new challenges

Sixth and last, don't be afraid to try new and creative ways to deal with old problems and new challenges, because some of the most wonderful methods of teaching basic understandings unfold in unique ways, and that is the creative part of creating a positive classroom! Pedro Noguera (1995) describes how an Oakland, California, junior high school dealt with a security-related matter in a novel way: The school board voted to hire not a security guard but a local grandmother to monitor students. Instead of relying on strip-searches and "instead of using physical intimidation to carry out her duties, this woman greets children with hugs" (p. 206). And when the hugs proved to be insufficient to maintain suitable behavior, instead of punishments "she admonishes them to behave themselves, saying she expects better behavior from them" (p. 206). Although some might chuckle at the seeming naïveté of hiring a grandmother instead of an armed guard, this junior high school was the only school in the district where no weapons were confiscated from students. Noguera also visited a high school where the principal closed the campus during lunchtime (for security reasons)

> . . . without installing a fence or some other security apparatus, but simply by communicating with students about other alternatives for purchasing food so that they no longer felt it necessary to leave for meals. Now the students operate a campus store that both teachers and students patronize. (p. 206)

High school teachers can be creative in promoting basic understandings. Using the content of her school's regular curriculum, secondary school English teacher Barbara Stanford (1995) integrates conflict management into her unit on the short story. Her unit begins with activities in which the students look at conflict in their lives. They develop a safe "fictional conflict diary" for a fictitious student, and the class constructs entries to that group diary each day. At the same time, each student keeps his or her own diary, analyzing ways he or she addresses conflict, and contributes to the class diary. Gradually the teacher leads the students to look at conflict outside themselves; through the short story they explore ways to deal with conflict. The class uses role plays and empathy-building activities. Stanford's work has been successful, particularly because she extends the learning outside the classroom to the students' lives.

In summary, here is a mini-checklist for supporting basic understandings (rules that teach):

Make sure your classroom feels safe to your students.

Work toward building a unique and special identity for your classroom.

Model empathic behavior at all times—toward students and other adults.

Make basic understandings stick at a personal level by actively and concretely teaching and practicing them.

Praise and give acknowledgment to students for acting humanely, but never reward them for doing so.

Seek innovative and creative ways to promote basic understandings.

In *Miracle in East Harlem,* author Sy Fliegel (1993) summarizes these points quite well: "Treat a classroom full of inner-city kids like a bunch of uneducable future criminals, and they won't let you down. Treat them with love, respect, and dignity, however, and watch them bloom" (p. 24). In "A Last Word," Daniel Goleman emphasizes how important it is for teachers and schools to actively teach students fundamentals of emotional competence like handling anger and resolving conflicts positively. "It takes a village to raise a child" may be a sweet and fetching sentiment, but American villages are gone, and its communities are fast disappearing. In today's America, it takes a positive school and classroom to help raise our children and adolescents. These classrooms are that village, that realistic community. They are places where strangers can still come together and do constructive things, bound by their mutual interest in young people and in their neighborhood. Goleman concludes by saying:

> Given the crises we find ourselves and our children facing, and given the quantum of hope held out by courses in emotional literacy, we must ask ourselves: Shouldn't we be teaching these most essential skills for life to every child—now more than ever? And if not now, when? (1995, p. 287)

Particularly for those students whose home and neighborhood lives are filled with cynicism and violence, schools and classrooms can hold the necessary conditions to disrupt the cycle of violence-to-incarceration-to-recidivism for many Americans. America's schools can no longer carry on as quasi-police, judicial, or penal institutions. There is far too much other more pressing and constructive work to do with our young people.

PART II

Four Dimensions of Positive Classrooms

Showing Students You Care and That They Will Be Successful

The Spiritual Dimension

n my companion text *Great Teaching: What Matters Most in Helping Students Succeed*, I describe *caring* and *efficacy*, two key qualities that "directly influence student success and student achievement" (2004, p. 47). These two qualities comprise the spiritual dimension of positive classrooms, and they are not merely important: They are essential elements of those classrooms. Let's examine caring. At first, caring may seem to be a no-brainer, an all-too-obvious given: "Sure, we should care about our students." But in the context of the positive classroom, caring is much more than a nice and sweet feeling. It is an attitude and tone of acceptance and loving regard that is fundamental to students' feeling safe, feeling valued, being motivated to learn, believing they will learn, and *actually achieving*, both academically and socially. More than a mere classroom nicety, caring powerfully contributes to a teacher's ability to work with students, having a "significant effect" on students' "academic performance and behavior" (Perez, 2000, p. 103). Putting the spiritual dimension shoe on the other foot, ask yourself how hard *you* would work with or for someone you felt did not like you or did not care about you.

Caring teachers show their care by building and maintaining a person-to-person relationship with their students. When students say that a teacher "treats students like individuals," they are talking about caring.

We teachers show whether or not we care by the ways we model empathy or its flip side: cruelty. I used to teach in a classroom across the hall from a teacher who relished blaming students, often to their faces. I'd overhear her tell another teacher, "Trevor got just what he deserved," or, "Danielle was absent the day I taught it, so she has nobody to blame but herself." Young people learn empathy—and aggression—very powerfully from the models we provide.

Caring is also shown in the ways we talk to our students. Do we speak as if they are simpletons? Do we say "Thank you" and "Please" when we are talking to them? Are we careful to separate the *behavior/misbehavior* from the *student?* (That same teacher also liked the word *always:* "Why do you *always* do that?" "Why do you *always* interrupt?" "Why do you *always* forget your homework?") We teachers show caring by modeling reflective listening—looking at students who are talking to us, and not interrupting students or finishing their sentences for them. Getting to know—and using—students' first names is also a sign they are important to us.

The spiritual dimension guides us to be sensitive to our students, even in ways that may seem unusual. For instance, even though the color red is traditionally used in grading papers, I say teachers should avoid using red pen and pencil in grading student work. Red always seemed such a hostile color, and I tossed out my red pens for good when I learned that one of my Korean students was distressed upon seeing I had written his name in red. I learned from his classmate that seeing one's name in red suggests impending death in Korean culture. After apologizing to my precious little student, I bought a large supply of green Bic pens. For the past thirty years I have used only green ink or lead in all my written work as a teacher—for grading exams, for writing notes to students, and for other communication.

At a deeper level, we show caring by teaching students how to resolve conflicts and by teaching and modeling appropriate ways to deal with frustration—what to do when something is not working. Most people *feel* empathy, but many need to learn how to *show* empathy in interactions with others. It works well to overtly tell students you expect them to respect each other, to respect us teachers (yes, even the ones they are not crazy about!), and to respect themselves. (Acclaimed author Noah ben Shea and I coauthored a text, *A Compass for the Classroom* [2005], which offers suggestions and ideas that can help teachers stay on track while at the same time allowing their students to see their caring.)

Among students in general—and among minority students in particular—a belief that a teacher does not care for his or her students can be like a death sentence. No matter how skillful the teacher may be and no matter how experienced or dedicated he or she is, if the students sense that

that teacher does not care about them or dislikes them, student success becomes a difficult or impossible goal to reach.

The other key teacher quality of the spiritual dimension is *efficacy*. Efficacy is the belief that one will be successful in a given task or pursuit, whether it be teaching, biking, reading, learning a language, kicking a field goal, or anything else pursuable. Teacher efficacy creates and incubates student efficacy, which is supported by student EQ. A student's EQ promotes social intelligence—a factor that has great impact on that student's success in life, both inside and outside the classroom. Teachers help student EQ grow by creating a setting where students will be successful at tasks that are challenging—and worth the challenge.

What are some of the best actions teachers can employ to build student efficacy? I have settled on four practices that stand out from my personal experience as a teacher and principal and from my reading of the professional education literature. These interventions set the foundation for student success and help build student EQ.

First, a teacher communicates instructional expectations for students

California high school teacher Jaime Escalante, portrayed in the film *Stand and Deliver* (Musca & Menéndez, 1998), was horrified at the low expectations his colleagues held for their students. His high (but not unrealistic) expectations for success—clearly conveyed—dramatically influenced his students' achievement, so that a majority of his inner-city high school students were accepted into advanced-placement college-level courses. It is no surprise that student behavior in his classroom also improved in response to those high academic expectations.

Second, a teacher builds efficacy by conveying enthusiasm for the subject he or she is teaching

Indeed, enthusiasm has been identified in many studies as the most significant characteristic of an effective teacher. Teacher enthusiasm not only positively affects student behavior, but it improves student achievement as well. Enthusiasm is shown in many ways: a "Let's find out" attitude, tone of voice, moving around the classroom, and perhaps most of all, sharing and articulating interest in the subject. Jaime Escalante gave his students "ganas," a *desire* to be successful. He was not afraid to show students he was interested in math, sharing his enthusiasm by coming up with novel and interesting approaches to common math problems. It is also important to note that he made the classroom safe for students to express their enthusiasm, too.

Third, a teacher builds student efficacy by holding students accountable for their work

Once due dates and requirements are clearly established, the teacher holds students to those dates and requirements, giving reasonable reminders along the way. When students are held accountable for their work, the quality and quantity of their work rise, and there is a seriousness of purpose in the classroom.

Fourth, a teacher builds student efficacy by teaching students' *attributions*

Attribution teaching is something I discovered quite by accident years ago as an inner-city teacher. After a field trip, we returned to our classroom. Feeling really good about how everything had gone, I sat before my class and told them—in all sincerity—how impressed I had been with their conduct. Indeed, I said, they were the best sixth-grade class I'd ever had. More important than the reward value of my praise were the specific attributions I gave them: I told them how maturely they had behaved, and how they had conducted themselves as if they had pride in being part of the group. I pointed to examples: How they had behaved traveling to and from the New York City subway—walking but not running into the subway car, allowing a parent with a baby stroller to go through the turnstile first, sitting and talking quietly inside the subway car, a few of them even giving up their seats to several developmentally challenged adults. Wow. I told them how I'd seen other adults smiling at our class, and how one had told me, "What a nice group. . . . What high school are you from?" ("Can you believe it?" I asked my sixth-grade students. "They thought you were *high school students!*") Days and weeks after our field trip, I noticed my students were indeed acting more mature in the classroom. By teaching them their attributions (calling them mature, considerate, adultlike), I was telling them *who they were*, and they unconsciously and consciously worked to live up to those positive attributions.

Thus, years before I heard the term "attribution teaching," I realized how powerful it is to teach students *who they are*. It's important to point out that I wasn't trying to *persuade* them ("You *should* act mature"), nor was I *rewarding* them ("I'm giving you all a party because your behavior was so mature!"). I was simply *teaching them believable truths about themselves*. Perhaps the strongest argument for using attribution teaching is that the flip side of students' belief that they will succeed is a debilitating and ugly phenomenon called "learned helplessness," where students' experiences result in failure so often that they come to expect they will be unsuccessful no matter what effort is exerted. I hate to think how many teachers are promoting learned helplessness in students *directly*, by telling them how horrible or stupid they are, and/or *indirectly*, by overpowering or disempowering them, preventing them from having any say about what they learn or do during their school day.

THREE AXIOMS FOR BUILDING STUDENT EFFICACY

Let's look inside terms like *expectations, enthusiasm, accountability,* and *attributions* for a moment and realize they all connect to, spring from, and generate student success. I have identified three axioms—each under the control of all teachers—that underlie this understanding. These axioms are perhaps the most essential truths I know of regarding success in teaching students. What has student success to do with positive classrooms? Plenty.

Axiom #1: Students who feel successful are seldom behavior problems.

Axiom #2: To feel successful, students must actually *be* successful.

Axiom #3: To actually be successful, a student must first do something of value.

Let's look at the first axiom.

Axiom #1: Students who *feel successful* are seldom behavior problems.

All but the most hardened of teachers want their students to feel successful. Ever since the very first student flunked the very first exam, teachers have been concerned about helping students do better in school. Some teachers try to achieve this by making school more user-friendly: They seek to be more permissive and more cordial. Others respond by being stricter or by demanding that students follow a rigid structure. Both responses miss the mark. Permissiveness and authoritarianism are extremes, and although they may help the teacher feel better liked or more in control, they do not work toward greater success for students. What, then, really works? How can our students feel successful?

Axiom #2: To feel successful, students must actually *be successful.*

Acceptance, praise, and rewards from the teacher may temporarily make a student feel good, but they do not translate directly into student success. Even getting high grades (the traditional indicator of school success) does not necessarily boost a student's sense of success. On the other hand, when a student actually experiences success, that experience creates an effect far more powerful than any teacher's words, grades, or rewards. But in order to experience genuine success, the student must *do* something.

Axiom #3: To actually be successful, a student must first *do something of value.*

Feelings of success come when a student actually does something of value—participating, performing, creating, practicing, designing, producing, carrying out an experiment, finishing an assignment, or any of hundreds of other activities. In the end, what the student does will have a greater impact on how successful the student is (and feels he or she is) than what the teacher knows, says, or believes. This is the heart of student efficacy—a student's belief that he or she will be successful in a given pursuit or endeavor.

My three axioms are particularly relevant to all students in elementary school through high school, because in this age span students are absorbed by activity and by the need to do things well. Erik Erikson's (1963) stage of "Industry Versus Inferiority" arises in the early elementary school years: Students are concerned with the quality of their handiwork: *how well* they have done. Anyone who has taught second-graders has seen them waving their papers, seeking the teacher's attention and approval: "Is this right?" they ask. "Is this good?" they wonder. In Erikson's next stage, "Identity Versus Role Confusion" (1963, pp. 261–263), these success experiences are internalized, brought together to comprise one's sense of "inner sameness and continuity," of having a unified, unique self; an *identity.* Doing well in school really does matter to students, even those who pretend otherwise. Sadly, students quickly learn to label winners and losers in the classroom: Elementary school students as young as kindergarten age can readily tell you who the good kids and the bad kids are. At any middle school or high school, students can promptly name the winners (usually, athletes and popular kids) and losers (unpopular kids, rejects, and worse). But being in neither category—everyone else—is no cause for great celebration, either.

High school students need to be successful not one bit less than younger children. To me, it is one of contemporary education's greatest ironies that high schools seem less focused on ensuring success for their students than elementary schools. It would seem to be more important, because older students *require* success in order to form their adult identities. Personal success in high school shapes students' futures and their sense of competency. It determines what students' post–high school plans will be, what careers they will pursue as adults, with whom they will associate, and how the adult world will come to value who they are. Again, I am amazed that, except for those given to sports and academic elites, there is not a broader range of success experiences available to American high school students, given the enormous implications of those experiences for life satisfaction and positive transition to adulthood.

In conclusion, the spiritual dimension is addressed by using caring and efficacy in the very best ways possible. This entails *planning* for all students to experience success. I would go so far as to recommend that teachers not allow the first day of class to pass without each student's experiencing success, even if by way of a modest task or achievement. We are supportive by our body language—the way we appear to our students. This includes using active listening and eye contact. A key element of the spiritual dimension is restoration: No matter what has happened, once an issue has been settled, the student is restored, returned to the good graces of all. There is an end point after which the problem is put in the past, making a clear pathway for students to *come back*—to return to a positive equilibrium with the teacher, with the other students, and with themselves.

Setting Up a Safe and Productive Learning Environment

The Physical Dimension

Schools and classrooms are artificial learning environments. Think about this: We seat a student for 6 hours in an overheated room bathed in fluorescent light, among 20 to 30 (or more) other eager, restless, or bored students, and insist that they all stay seated and/or keep quiet for long periods of time during that day!

Of course, many teachers work to overcome this dreary physical scenario through the use of, for example, differentiated instruction, as well as more highly interactive cooperative learning approaches. Nevertheless, too many students still face each day in what can be described as an institutional warehouse, and in some worse cases, a prison, discouraging to the spirit and destructive of any curiosity and enthusiasm to learn.

Are these adequate situations for learning? Is learning even possible under such circumstances? The answers are obvious. There is hope. It starts with you, a teacher who wants to make school a hospitable place for learning. Perhaps you have seen a teacher who accomplishes this with little things in his or her classroom: the teacher who uses his students' works—art, for example—to decorate a classroom, or the teacher who makes her classroom a safe place even when streets outside are dangerous, or the teacher whose imaginative setup of classroom furniture frees students from being anchored in a seat for hours at a time.

Teaching does not occur in a vacuum. It takes place somewhere. That somewhere, that environment (typically, the classroom), is the physical dimension of your positive classroom. Too many of us take the physical dimension for granted, or we ignore it. However, it is integral to the positive classroom because it directly impacts the other three dimensions. Prior to instruction, and before you plan for managerial issues, think about and then act on the classroom's physical environment that you and the students will occupy. Yes, there are limitations to what you can change: You cannot change the building, the size of the classroom, the number of students, or the social class and family income of the students you will have in that classroom. Yet there is much you can (and must) influence, ranging from the first impression someone gets upon entering the room to the comfort and safety experienced by the students. It takes a little thought and planning, but not much money or time.

Specifically, how can we set up the classroom to be a safe and productive learning environment? To begin, focus on these three areas: the nuts and bolts (desks, tables, bookcases, and that stuff), the human factor (how people will use the nuts and bolts), and the ambience (feeling of the room). As you read the following, have a pen and paper handy to make notes on your own physical environment.

THE NUTS AND BOLTS

First are the concrete, tangible, nuts-and-bolts considerations. Each student must have a place to work and a place to store his or her things. Decide whether your students will use desks or tables, and see if they are in good condition and appropriate for your students' use. The lighting should be strong enough to prevent eyestrain; heat should not put people to sleep, nor the lack of it allow icicles to grow on noses. How is the noise level? Is there a noisy or highly distracting condition emanating from within the school? Outside the school? There should also be no obvious safety problems, and this includes having adequate entrance and exit doorways.

THE HUMAN FACTOR

Consider the human factor. How will you and the students live together in this rather tight (or gaping) space for most of a year? How can you set it up to maximize the educational benefit for your students?

Essentially, students need to be able to see and hear you, and vice versa. No matter what type of classroom you run, your lines of sight and sound to all areas of the classroom must be unobstructed. In fact, you need clear lines of sight from many different parts of the classroom: the door, the teacher's desk, the chalkboard. Your students' lines of sight and sound count, too. Put yourself in their places: Are chalkboards and bulletin boards placed at their sight level? Are desks and tables the right size and height for your students?

Also essential is the idea that human beings have to move about. Will there be space for this to occur comfortably? Will people crash into one another? Potential behavior problems can be eliminated if traffic lanes are uncluttered and are as wide as possible.

There will be times when students stay put. At these times, you will want students to work in comfort, but beware of making things too comfortable, lest they fall asleep! (I have seen cushy sofas and plush-lined bathtubs in the classroom, which can rapidly bring on slumber.)

THE AMBIENCE

Think about the intangible, the ambience. *Ambience* is the French word for environment or surroundings—that unnamable feeling you experience upon setting foot in a room. It comes from everything—odors, humidity, ventilation, chalk dust, heat, cold, noise, echo, and quiet. They all come together to give a room a unique ambience. Walk in as a stranger a few times when the room is still new to you. Use all your senses: What strikes you? What feels good? What needs to be changed?

Using less than $100 worth of materials, New York City fourth-grade teacher Mary Sullivan treated her classroom to a makeover, with the help of California teacher and designer Frank Garcia. The makeover included colorful new bulletin board designs, an inviting reading center and book display, and a novel art learning center. It even included a special lightweight stool so Mary no longer had to perch herself on the edge of a desk or crouch uncomfortably as she worked with her students (Murray, 1994).

Do not discount the importance of ambience. Each room has its own feel, and that feel sends an immediate message to each person who visits for 6 minutes and to each captive who must occupy that room for 6 hours a day. Air fresheners are inexpensive; the natural air-freshening power of natural sunlight is even cheaper, and it freshens dark corners as well. Green foliage plants clean the air. (I have heard that spider plants remove carbon monoxide.) Teachers can invite the students to contribute to the ambience of the classroom. Flowers from your students' gardens are free. (Yes, even dandelions count. They grow all over New York City, Chicago, Los Angeles, and in other cities and towns across the country!)

USING THE PHYSICAL DIMENSION

In addition to setting up your room before classes begin, consider how the room will be used to support instruction later. For example, by using flexible seating you can have students easily move into groups when your instruction plans call for cooperative group work. Also consider other practical aspects: Will the layout of your classroom suit your teaching style and needs? Are supplies convenient? Will you have to move aside two boxes of obsolete software each time you wish to use the supply closet? Do students have to step over backpacks to reach the door? Are supplies and books on shelves within easy reach?

A key way that the physical classroom supports teaching and learning is in helping students, regardless of age, feel *symbolic identification* with the classroom; that is, students have an investment in, or ownership of, the classroom. Symbolic identification means that students can see something about themselves in the physical classroom—student essays posted on the walls, a bulletin board asking viewers to match the picture of the student with the picture of the student's pet, photos of the class play, or a computer monitor that plays a slide show of the class picnic. I always feel an opportunity has been lost when I see classrooms decorated exclusively with store-bought, professionally manufactured decorations (or worse, bare walls). They may be attractive, but they add zero to the students' ability to connect with the classroom, and in effect, with each other. Instead, teachers can promote symbolic identification by using student works within and near the classroom; drawing attention to student works; encouraging students to share their works, papers, and projects with others in the room; and giving students a role in designing the classroom's decor.

Finally, you will need to consider corrective interventions: How will you use the physical classroom when you must react, after a problem arises? For example, will you have a time-out area, a quiet, private spot inside the classroom? If you set up such an area, it should be out of the way of heavy traffic, yet not completely isolated from you or the class. I find it best to use the time-out area not as a personal prison, but as a quiet place where students can get that work done, or think about what happened and how they might handle things differently next time. Don't use an in-class space for more serious infractions, or if the student is still in a state of froth and turmoil, likely to continue his or her eruption. For those cases, have arranged ahead of time an out-of-classroom place where the student can work, recover, and settle down, a place that is supervised and safe for the student and others. This is especially relevant for older students. High school teachers would do well to stop sending students into the hall after a behavioral infraction or annoying episode. If the student is injured or injures another while outside the classroom, there will be a serious question of how wise it was to eject the student in the first place. In a positive classroom, ejection of a student should be a rare event. When it is necessary, having a designated, safe destination and a clear assignment for the student is always a much better alternative than simply banishing the student into the hallway.

In conclusion, it pays to remember that although there are times every teacher must react by making corrective interventions, and that teachers should be prepared for those times, preventive and supportive interventions are always preferable for both the student and the teacher.

Teaching
So Students
Stay Focused
and Learn

The Instructional Dimension

In addressing the instructional dimension, we take a look at how to teach so that students stay focused and learn. Instruction is not usually included in considerations of classroom management, yet the way a teacher teaches—what he or she says and does and leads the students to do—is central to the positive classroom, from the perspectives of both social development and student achievement. "What do teachers do that works best?" is an often-asked question in the practice of teaching. Indeed, I have been asking that question for over 35 years—asking it of the professional literature, asking it by way of teacher observations conducted as a school principal, and most recently, asking it by way of formal classroom observation research studies. The literature holds that there are "specific instructional procedures" (also known as "skills") that teachers use to "lead to increased achievement and student engagement in the classrooms" (Rosenshine & Stevens, 1986, p. 376). Student engagement is aided when the traditional one-way lecture gives way to more interactive teaching styles, leading to student success (Gettinger, 1995; Gettinger & Stoiber, 1999).

In addition to completing classroom observations in my role as school principal, over the past 5 years I have done structured observations of teachers in over 100 classrooms in the U.S. and abroad, and have noted which teacher-instruction practices have a positive effect—the best impact—on both student achievement and social development (positive behavior). These practices, which I call key teacher skills, are the eight I would select if I had to pick the most important skills a teacher should master. (Note that I describe each of these skills in detail in my companion text *Great Teaching: What Matters Most in Helping Students Succeed* [2004].) These key teacher skills include:

Preparation. Thinking about—and planning for—what each person in the classroom will do. Involves:

- identifying content and student needs
- lesson, unit, and yearly planning
- planning for student success

Attention. Guiding students to establish and maintain focus. Involves:

- establishing opening focus
- maintaining ongoing focus
- expecting all learners to participate

Clarity. Striving to be clear in communication with students. Involves:

- giving clear instructions
- using precise terminology
- having students restate instructions before starting assignments

Questioning. Asking lots of questions and inviting students to ask questions. Involves:

- asking opening, focusing, and probing questions
- frequent questioning, and questioning all students over time
- inviting student questions

Monitoring. Overseeing student work as it is being created. Involves:

- maintaining appropriate proximity to learners
- "with-it"ness—awareness of what is happening in the classroom
- overlapping—not breaking instructional flow for distractions

Feedback. Providing students with immediate and specific assessment. Involves:

- giving specific feedback information
- giving immediate feedback, as soon after the behavior as possible
- giving ongoing feedback as continuous assessment

Summarizing. Leading students to review and recap what they have learned. Involves:

- using formative summaries by teacher and students
- "setting the table" for the next class meeting
- using reviews to deepen understanding

Reflection. Contemplating instruction that has taken place and that will take place. Involves:

- reviewing past instruction, using evidence of learner success or failure
- carrying out long-term evidence-based review of prior instruction
- engaging in reflective conversations with other teachers and students

Thinking specifically about how teaching helps create the positive classroom, I have put together a list of 10 differentiated instruction strategies you can implement immediately in your classroom to ensure student success. Although there are many definitions of *differentiated instruction*, we all agree that differentiated instruction is a way of modifying instruction to suit the needs of students with various learning styles, interests, areas of knowledge, abilities, and skill levels within a given classroom. This requires that teachers use a variety of effective teaching strategies. Special education teachers can be extremely helpful advising you in ways to differentiate curriculum, since they do just that with their students; they can advise you about the instructional needs of students in general as well as those of specific students. Differentiated instruction strategies can be used with all grade levels, preschool through high school (and I have used some in my college classrooms as well).

As you consider the list of strategies I have provided, think about axiom #3, introduced earlier in the chapter on the spiritual dimension: To actually be successful, a student must first do something of value. Thus, no matter what the grade level, age, gender, or other status of the student, in order for differentiated instruction to pay off, the student must—fundamentally—be proactively involved in your instruction.

Suggested activity: For each month from mid-September through June, pick one of the following strategies and work at it for the entire month. At the end of the month, reflect on how well you carried out that strategy.

Ten Differentiated Instruction Strategies That Promote a Positive Classroom

1. Gear your instruction to the correct level of difficulty.

2. Break instruction into smaller learnings.

3. Build patterning and association into each lesson.

4. Ensure success by giving your students the most precious commodity you have: time.

5. Have students work in cooperation, not competition.

6. Ensure success by getting to know your students' strengths.

7. Perhaps most important of all, teach students to take responsibility for their learning.

8. Increase student interest.

9. Provide assessment that helps the student and informs the teacher.

10. Work toward smooth flow and lively pacing.

---

1. First (and basic to differentiated instruction), gear your instruction to the correct level of difficulty. Especially with new teachers, too much time is spent in instruction that is either too simplistic or beyond students' ability. Try to aim your classroom instruction at what I call "the point of just manageable difficulty"—a point slightly beyond your students' current achievement level. Start by getting a sense of where they are. For example, this evening, before you put away that stack of checked/graded student work, skim the pile of papers in your hand, trying to get a sense of the overall difficulty level. Was the work too easy? Too hard? Make adjustments accordingly. Yet, be patient: Even the most experienced teachers find it challenging to locate that point of just manageable difficulty! And that point will be different for different students. Grouping students for instruction is a way of getting a handle on the level of difficulty for a whole class of students.

2. Break instruction into smaller learnings. First, get the big idea, or what Carol Ann Tomlinson calls "the essential concepts, principles, and skills of each subject" (1999, p. 9). For example, teaching students to use a computer requires that they first learn how to use a mouse, but the key here is to first determine whether they already know how to use that mouse. Similarly, get a sense of how well students have mastered basic keyboard orientation before tackling the Internet. If you equip students with prerequisite tools, mastering the task and attaining success become doable. Formative (continuous) assessment is an integral element here, allowing you to track students' ongoing progress. (*Weaving Science Inquiry and Continuous Assessment* by Carlson, Humphrey, & Reinhardt [2003] is an excellent guide to continuous assessment in science and other subjects.)

3. Build patterning and association into each lesson. At one time, we can store only about 4 or 5 bits of new information in our minds. Patterning can help out. Let's say there are 20 new vocabulary words to memorize—in science, math, or social studies. Teach students to pattern them—sometimes called "chunking" them—by dividing them into four or five subgroups. They could be grouped by initial letter (hemlock, hickory, hawthorn, holly, hornbeam), by mnemonics (Argentina, Brazil, Chile), or by other patterns. Challenge high school students to come up with their own patterns.

Association means connecting new concepts and learnings to what students already know. Have students build on what they know by comparing it to, contrasting it with, or making analogies of it to new material. For instance, when introducing the concept of multiplication, guide elementary students to discover that multiplication (unfamiliar, new concept) is really the same as old, familiar addition. The strange new algorithm 3×5 is nothing more than adding $5 + 5 + 5$. A high school science teacher can use association by connecting Bernoulli's principle to the lift of an airplane wing or to the curve of a pitched baseball.

4. Ensure success by giving your students the most precious commodity you have: time. Avoid sound bite fragmentation! Provide adequate time for students to process—to do something with—what they have learned. Research shows us that when students process what they have learned, they not only stay focused for a longer period of time, but they also retain more. We also know that in order to differentiate instruction, we must acknowledge that different students process information at different rates. Yes, some students process more slowly, and these are the ones most at risk in a "rush-rush" classroom.

How can you avoid fragmentation? When asking questions, use *wait time*: Simply wait quietly for 3 to 5 seconds after asking a question. (Some teachers wait less than 1 second after asking a question before they respond, immediately answering their own question!) Wait time increases student involvement, allows richer student responses, and brings slower students into classroom instruction. Whole-block scheduling (longer periods of instruction) is used in some middle and high schools to allow students more time to process what they are learning.

Speaking of time, you can ensure success by eliminating unintended "hang-loose" time. This is when students have no idea what to do, and are thus at great risk for engaging in unproductive or antisocial behavior. A strategy I have used with success is "do-now" work. When my active middle school students entered the classroom, I already had a do-now assignment on the chalkboard. This cut down on dawdling and mischief. With do-now work, students waste no time getting started (it's nonnegotiable!). But you need not have everyone doing the same thing at the same time. Some teachers have students work on journals as soon as they enter. Others have students work in groups checking their work, or working at an activity center. Either way, do-now work helps students become focused and self-sufficient, and it also allows the teacher time to address administrative tasks, and to put out fires that some students bring to school within themselves.

How else can you help students process what they have learned? Have them teach! Asking students to teach other students provides the students-as-teachers with an incredibly powerful way to master the material. Rotate assignments to make sure each student gets opportunities to be a student-as-teacher and a student-as-student!

5. Have students work in cooperation, not competition. Define *successful* as being fruitful and productive, not winning out over someone else. In baseball or tennis, when one team wins, the other must lose, but learning to read and write, for example, is not suited to such zero-sum methods. Assign as many "A"s as you honestly can, when student work has met the criteria. The criteria should not depend on the number of others who also did well (which defeats the purpose of using criterion-based assessment).

Robert Slavin of Johns Hopkins University has written extensively and persuasively about the value of cooperative learning, where students work together in heterogeneous (mixed ability) teams to master material presented by the teacher. Moreover, cooperative learning directly contributes to the positive classroom. Slavin acknowledges that "most cooperative learning classrooms are well behaved, because students are motivated to learn and are actively engaged in learning activities" (1990, p. 115).

Evaluate more but judge less. Avoid making unnecessary good/bad, pass/fail achievement distinctions. Such black-and-white judgments are inappropriate for introductory lessons, cooperative writing projects, poetry reading, science exhibits, construction of computer databases, community action projects, political polling, sculpting, and hundreds of other endeavors. Sometimes we teachers spend more time judging than teaching. To paraphrase French essayist Joseph Joubert (1928), our students "need models rather than critics."

6. Ensure success by getting to know your students' strengths. Howard Gardner's (1983, 1993) multiple intelligences (MI) theory is a godsend to differentiated instruction. It frees teachers from the old dictum that insisted "all students be on the same page in the same book at the same time." Instead, Gardner has drawn our attention to ways in which our students are different, ways that they have unique strengths.

Consider using Gardner's multiple intelligences as a means to teach to that wider range of student capabilities. Gardner's intelligences include linguistic, logical-mathematical, spatial, musical, bodily-kinesthetic, interpersonal, intrapersonal, naturalist, and existential intelligences. Schools have traditionally emphasized the first two (linguistic and logical-mathematical) intelligences. Recognizing and teaching to the other intelligences opens exciting new areas for student success—brainstorming, connecting, composing, drawing, organizing, synthesizing, building, rebuilding, designing, predicting, and hundreds of others. (For superb classroom applications of Gardner's MI theory, see Thomas Armstrong's *Multiple Intelligences in the Classroom*, Second Edition [2000].)

Assessment is a starting point for differentiating instruction. Instead of using only those reading-and-math-heavy diagnostic tests, why not start the school year by getting to know student likes and dislikes? What are your students good at? Have older students complete an interest inventory, based on emotional intelligence or the multiple intelligences. Ask young students to list things they do well outside of school. (How exciting it is to start the school year by letting your teacher know what you do well and what you like to do!) One of my fifth-grade students struggled for years with reading. In a previous school, Bekah had been—in her mother's words—"remediated to death." By talking with Mom, we learned that Bekah had a hidden talent—she was a gifted photographer. Bekah had a shoe box full of stunning close-up color photograph prints she had taken of flowers. What an exhibit Bekah presented at that year's PTA carnival!

7. Perhaps most important of all, teach students to take responsibility for their learning. Nothing will certify you as an excellent teacher more than your teaching students to be independent learners who are accountable for their work, learning, and progress. Too many of us teachers require our students to be too dependent on us, too used to being spoon-fed. As a result, students will define success in school simply as their ability to follow directions and repeat back to the teacher what they think the teacher wants to hear. Although following directions is a legitimate skill, useful for convergent tasks and some types of problem solving, a broad, curriculum-wide emphasis on following directions stands in the way of a student's taking responsibility for his or her learning, and can destroy intrinsic motivation, to say nothing of creativity. Given the current testing frenzy, U.S. schools emphasize compliance more than they have in the past. Hence, your encouragement and permission are needed to help students understand that it's okay for them to think on their own. Have students do freewrites, or compose music, art, or poetry, or do other personalized activities that are not necessarily in lockstep with state standards!

Another way to help students take responsibility is to see to it that their efforts are not in vain. There has to be some payoff at some point for each of us that includes more than a reward or avoidance of punishment. Here's why: When animals receive punishment that they cannot stop no matter what efforts they exert, they eventually stop exerting effort. This lack of effort is so strong that it remains, even later when the animal's efforts can stop the punishment (Seligman, 1975). In humans, this "learned helplessness" occurs when one's ongoing lack of control eventually results in a conviction that whatever is attempted will lead to failure. It's the direct opposite of self-efficacy, the belief that one's efforts are likely to result in success. But there's more to student success than getting rewarded or avoiding punishment. Students need to have the power to choose what form their efforts will take. Alfie Kohn (1993a, p. 11) emphasizes that "people are likely to persist at doing constructive things, like exercising, quitting smoking, or fighting cavities, *when they have some choice about the specifics of such programs* [italics added]."

Along the same lines, at times we teachers do so much for our students that it prevents their learning to do those things for themselves. When I taught music in a Brooklyn public school, I made up a music sheet with a tune for my fourth-grade song flute students to play. I handed it to the office for duplication, but it came back in my mailbox with a "See me" note from the principal.

"What was wrong with my music sheet?" I asked.

He told me. "You're doing too much for your students! Do your students know how to draw a G clef?" he asked.

"No, I don't think so," I admitted.

"Do they know how to write music notes yet? Whole notes? Half notes?"

"No, probably not."

"Then give them blank staff paper and have them learn to *write the notes and musical symbols themselves! Teach them!*" he implored.

He was right on target. Years later, as a principal myself, I repeated that same message to my teachers: "If you do too much for students, you rob them of the chance and desire to do for themselves." In today's schools, where rush-rush is the rule, we have to be especially careful that we don't cheat our students in the interest of saving time. If we are always providing room service, our students will never learn to cook for themselves. Think about how much you do for your students, and what part of it they can and should do for themselves. We don't want to turn our students into educational invalids.

As you teach, try to get comfortable involving your students in planning their day. For example, each morning I would give my students an overview of the day ahead. Some activities were not negotiable (opening exercises, testing, lunch, etc.), but others were flexible. "I'm thinking of spending more time on math this morning to give you more time to work on those fraction problems we began yesterday. That means our puppet show will come after lunch. Does that sound good?" I would ask the students, and I would be prepared to go with their thoughts if sound reasons were provided.

Contracting is another useful technique to help older elementary, middle, and high school students take responsibility for their learning. The student and teacher draw up a contract, which spells out requirements and time for completion, and both of them sign it.

8. Increase student interest. Perhaps no strategy is more obvious than (yet as frequently ignored as) this one. In all schools, students are compelled to do all they are told to do. While unquestioned compliance can make things work smoothly from the school's point of view, this compulsion also has a downside: It can cause us to forget the importance of student interest and motivation. My student teachers know that they may not start a lesson (with me sitting there) by telling their students, "Okay, open to page thirty-three," or, "Copy these problems from the board." Yes, students should do as they are told, but we must be very careful how we use our expectation that they will do so. We abuse our authority when we routinely demand complete compliance, especially when we ignore our students' engagement and interest. Hence, my student teachers start teaching a lesson by having their students bring to mind what they did yesterday, or by helping students make connections between what they already know and what today's learning promises to bring, or by providing some engaging event that serves as an opening hook (one student high school teacher put on a wig and opened science class by pretending to be Albert Einstein explaining his theory of relativity—everyone was on task for that class!). Educators have known for years that students who are interested in what they are doing will not only enjoy doing it, but will also sustain the activity for a longer period of time, become more deeply engaged in it, and retain more from it.

What else can teachers do to increase student interest? At least two things. First, *vary your instructional methods*. Instead of relying on one style of teaching (chalk-and-talk lecture, for example), involve students in a task where they can go hands-on: Demonstrate something, use simulation games, start with an engaging event (as above), or hold a guided class discussion. Students who are not inclined to speak up in class are usually the first to join in when an interesting class discussion begins. Similarly, students who are reticent about writing may be transformed when they are allowed to use a computer, for instance, when they write.

Another way to increase student interest is to *teach in multiple modalities*. Typically, the bulk of classroom time is devoted to verbal activities: lecturing, reading from a text, writing, and so forth. Yet, because words and numerals are highly abstract, they are harder to digest, especially for young children and slower learners. Instead of a blizzard of words and numerals, provide nonverbal stimuli such as demonstrations, pictures, and visual and multisensory activities that use concrete and pictorial modalities. These two modalities are best for "naive" learners—even adult learners—who have little prior knowledge of the idea or topic. Using pictures is better than using words, but the concrete—the real thing—is best of all. The pictorial mode works when concrete is not possible or practicable. Piaget and others remind us that the use of abstractions (words and numerals) is more suitable for older learners, as well as for learners who already have some prior understanding. Abstractions—no matter how colorful the words or pictures may be—cannot promote student understanding the way real objects and situations can, especially for younger learners, who profit from what Piaget calls "physical" and "logico-mathematical" (counting, sorting, combining) experiences (Kamii & DeClark, 1985, pp. 7–8).

Along the same lines, novelty and variety in classroom instruction can renew interest, but beware: Too much novelty or variety in a short period of time makes students passive observers. Television produces passivity precisely because it consists of novel, rapidly changing images; the viewer always remains a viewer and never becomes a doer. In the classroom, too much novelty may be more entertaining than substantial, moving the focus from the learner (student) to the performer (teacher).

Don't forget to use Gardner's multiple intelligences activities as another great way to increase student interest.

9. Provide assessment that helps the student and informs the teacher. Carol Tomlinson (2001) asks us to think of assessment as a road map as we plan for instruction. It's an apt analogy in two ways: Assessment can be an existing road map we refer to along our journey, and assessment can also be a road map we are constructing as we journey onward. The first analogy describes *formative* (ongoing) *assessment*, the second *informal assessment*, both central to the task of differentiating instruction.

Formative assessment (sometimes called "continuous assessment" or "formative evaluation") is assessment that is ongoing, asking, "Where are our students at this time?" According to assessment authority Grant Wiggins, "Our job is not only to uncover the big ideas of content . . . [but also includes] assessing as we teach, uncovering the learners' *understandings and misunderstandings* all along the way" (2005, p. 247). I like to use the analogy of "keeping our finger on the pulse of the class," on being in tune with whether or not students are "getting" what we think and hope they are getting.

Since the time of Socrates, asking students questions has been an efficient way for teachers to find out what students understand, and this helps the students themselves realize what they understand. Grant Wiggins (2005, pp. 248–249) adds the following eight engaging techniques to check on student understanding: using index cards for students to summarize what they do and do not understand; having students use hand signals (thumbs-up, thumbs-down); assigning one-minute essays; setting up a question box or board in the classroom where students may leave questions they do not understand; providing students with analogy prompts ("_____ is like _____ because _____"); having students create visual representations like web maps or concept maps; using follow-up probes like "Tell me more," "Give your reasons," and "Why?"; and doing "misconception checks," where students are presented with a predictable misconception about a concept or process and are asked to agree or disagree, explaining their responses.

We move on to *informal assessments*, which are contrasted with *formal assessments* like standardized tests, high-stakes assessments, and multiple-choice tests. Teachers today know that standardized tests have lately become more commonplace ("proliferated" is more like it) in American classrooms, driven by the push for a simple measure of accountability. Yet no matter how ubiquitous these tests may become, formal assessments can never be as helpful or as informative—to teachers, parents, or students—as informal assessments, especially for those of us wishing to capitalize on differentiated instruction. Informal assessments are those designed by you and sometimes by the students, and they can yield a tremendous amount of useful information. They are called informal because they *inform*, not because they are casual or nonchalant. When I began teaching in the inner-city schools of New York and tried to find out about my students' level of function—where they were academically—I had little to go on. All I had were standardized test results with lots of grade-equivalent numbers that helped me not at all in figuring out who knew what, or what I should teach to whom. Fortunately, my neighbor teacher introduced me to informal assessment. She suggested I start with book conferences: "Simply meet with your students one-to-one and talk about the book they read. Make up some questions ahead of time to test them, and have them come up with one or two good questions for you." This worked like a charm, especially for my students whose language and writing skills were limited. She also had me make up some informal math and reading tests, which I would use, reassuring my students that the tests were not going to be graded, simply to "help Mr. D. understand what he needs to teach you this year." Other informal assessments you can use include portfolios, writing samples, experience charts, projects, journal entries, keeping diaries, and authentic tasks. Authentic assessments can be powerful and real. For example, doing a multiple-choice test on solar or wind energy is not as powerful as actually designing and building a small model of a wind or solar generator. That model would be a more authentic test than a formal multiple-choice test because the model is more closely related to the real thing. Plus, it's a lot more fun.

Speaking of fun, both my younger and older students *loved* doing my September-to-June activity. In September, I would hold on to two assignments (usually a writing and a math exercise) the students had completed. In June, I would give the same assignments, which they would not remember having done back in September. After grading their later work, I would bring out what they had done in September. The looks on their faces were priceless as they held their works side by side. The differences were usually dramatic. (Some students even denied that the September work had been theirs!) Because it was *real*, this brief assessment activity served as a most persuasive form of feedback to students (and their teacher) that no standardized test could ever match.

10. Work toward smooth flow and lively pacing. Even though students are working at differentiated tasks and activities, the classroom as a whole should have a sense of tempo, a smooth flow. Sometimes teachers break that flow by making mountains out of molehills (for example, pointing to a paper on the floor and announcing, "This room is a mess! I am tired of seeing paper on the floor!"). This throws everyone off task. When extreme, it makes you an entertainer who is not very entertaining. Interruptions from bells, from the office, and from student misbehavior all destroy flow. You cannot do much about the bells, but students are another matter: Do not reprimand or even look at a student who is seeking to interrupt as you are teaching. Hold out your hand ("Stop") or an index finger ("One minute") to the interrupter, without taking your attention from the student who is talking to you. Try to follow through on your sentences, and when you are giving instructions, have students wait until you are finished before you field their questions.

Like capable automobile drivers who keep their visual focal points constantly moving from the road, to the mirror, to the speedometer, and back to the road, teachers must be aware of what is happening in the classroom. My dear Aunt Flora, who began teaching before the Great Depression, used to say that "A good teacher has eyes in the back of her head." At times, this requires *dovetailing*—doing two things at once. Years later I saw my aunt as a principal, speaking to a class of sixth-graders in her New York City elementary school. As she talked to the class, she approached Aaron, who was noisily spinning a pencil on his desk. Without pausing at all, or breaking eye contact with the class, Aunt Flora simply touched Aaron's desk with her fingertip as she walked past. Aaron immediately stopped playing with the pencil as she continued talking to the class. I was amazed by the smooth and economical way she handled the situation.

New teachers tend to have a problem with pacing, either dragging or going too fast. Both extremes cause problems: Too fast = confusing, confusion = boredom, and boredom = misbehavior. Too slow is just as bad: Dragging = boredom, and boredom = misbehavior.

Appropriate pacing is achieved by being sensitive to the pulse of the class, then moving ever so slightly faster than that pulse (like a surfer, perhaps, riding the crest of a wave). Probably the best technique to help you travel at the right instructional pace is to ask questions as you teach. Student responses to your questions will give you an accurate pulse count of the group. This will help you sense if you are losing some of the class to boredom and should be moving on.

You can enliven your teaching by having students do something different. Asking "How are plants and molds alike?" may cause some students to think, but saying, "Turn to your partner, and take two minutes to come up with three ways that plants and molds are alike" will cause all to think *and* to do something productive, and will keep the pace lively. By asking your students to do something active (and fun) like talking to a partner, you have instantly involved them in learning and banished boredom.

Or, without setting a time limit, ask students to brainstorm and write down three ways that plants and molds *differ*. Tip: In most activities like this, do not wait for all students to be finished before you move on. By that time, the ones who finished first are bored, and perhaps disengaged. Instead, move your eyes over the class, and when about half the class has finished, tell the entire group to finish up what they are working on. Then move on, having them share their brainstorm results with a partner (this will allow those who were not done to catch up without having the whole group wait). Again, keep things moving. Even set a time limit for sharing: "I'm going to give you three minutes to share brainstorms. Ready? Start!"

Keep to your word. You do not have to call time at exactly 3 minutes to the nanosecond, but when you do call time, mean it. Do not give in to "I'm not done!" protests. Help those students find time to finish later on.

Now, look back over the list of 10 strategies.

Pick one strategy and work at it for one month.

If you have a mentor, a buddy teacher, or another trusted colleague, ask him or her to observe your teaching and help monitor your progress toward mastery of the strategies that you need to address.

Managing a Smooth-Running Classroom

The Managerial Dimension

For many teachers, the managerial dimension is synonymous with classroom management itself. Indeed, it consists of planning and keeping up with all the noninstructional routines that are so important to a smooth-running classroom. These routines, which include those related to student behavior and misbehavior, involve considerations like: How will the teacher plan—lay the groundwork—for teaching positive student behavior? How will the teacher support and maintain that behavior? And the crucial consideration: What should the teacher do in response to student misbehavior?

In order to form a positive classroom, teachers approach the managerial dimension in three ways by making interventions I call *preventive*, *supportive*, and *corrective*, or in other words, before the fact, during the fact, and after the fact. Although teachers tend to focus on after-the-fact correctives (they worry about what to do if so-and-so does or says such-and-such), it is the preventive and supportive interventions that hold the most promise in creating a positive classroom. Being in a corrective mode will be necessary at times, but it is not the best place to be. At workshops I lead, I always get a question along the lines of, "Okay, Dr. Bob. What do I do if a student picks up his chair and throws it at me?" I always answer, "Duck."

Read through the following section to gain an understanding of each managerial intervention.

PREVENTIVE INTERVENTION: BEFORE THE FACT

Most new teachers (and nonteachers) are surprised to discover how much work goes into teaching, especially the work that is largely invisible—the work done prior to instruction, an essential part of managing a smooth-running classroom. Naturally, we teachers cannot anticipate every specific behavior and misbehavior that may occur. After all, we are working with somewhat unpredictable humans, not fairly predictable machines. But we can and must anticipate *situations* that are likely to develop. From a preventive viewpoint, this means getting on top of the situation. Early on, and long before you *must* do so, find out about basic school procedures, including the school's policies. What are they? What do they require of you?

Typically there are policies that address routine areas like school trips, school closings, fire drills, student arrival and dismissal, dress requirements, book selection, and so forth. However, and more so in today's climate of fear, school districts also have specific policies pertaining to drugs, alcohol, tobacco, sexual harassment, corporal punishment, HIV/AIDS, and violence. In fact, most schools today follow some form of violence prevention policy or program. These programs involve teachers in their implementation, and include prevention curricula, direct instruction, or training for students that includes "therapeutic activity" involving counselors, social workers, or psychologists. Violence prevention also involves a "review, revision, or monitoring" of schoolwide discipline practices and procedures (United States Department of Education, 1998, p. 24). In any event, as teachers, we are very much a key link in a school's violence prevention chain. Thus you will need to familiarize yourself with the school's policies. Yes, some school districts have hundreds of policies, so see if there is a policy manual for teachers as well as one for parents. If so, read them thoroughly. If neither is available, discuss the matter with the principal, because as I mentioned earlier, you will be held accountable for what those policies mandate. If you disagree with a policy, do not simply ignore it. Get together with others who share your disagreement

At the classroom level, being on top of the situation means laying the groundwork. Even before you meet them, get to know who your students are. There should be a folder for each student containing his or her permanent records. Skim the records and look for special-needs students, learning what health and educational accommodations will be needed for them. Find out about custody arrangements. Get information on any behavior problems and antisocial behavior students have shown in the past. Look at the positive, too: Which students will be helpful peer models of prosocial behavior for other students? Think about some of the classroom procedures you want to institute. What will your students do each day (aside from their learning activities)? What limits will be important to set that will help prevent behavior and management problems? What limits and procedures will you institute to help your students feel physically and emotionally safe in your room?

What can you do to lay the groundwork that will guide student behavior? Are you prepared to face students who may openly mock or challenge expectations for behavior? In these ways, *preventive* reaches ahead into the *supportive* and *corrective* areas, asking you to think about what you need to do to maintain positive behavior (supportive) and what you might do if confronted with minor to serious misbehavior (corrective). The checklists in Part III can help you gain an overview of specific preventive actions teachers can take.

Remember: If preventive interventions are the *work* of teaching (and they are), then supportive interventions are the *joy* of teaching.

SUPPORTIVE INTERVENTION: DURING THE FACT

To me, this area is the really exciting part of setting up and running a positive classroom. Through supportive interventions, we can work our magic with our students, really making our classrooms wonderful places for them (and us) to be. In using supportive interventions, teachers model and encourage the behaviors they seek to have students emulate while *supporting* students' efforts to achieve those important behaviors. To me, supportive interventions are where we teachers can do our very best work in helping make the world (community, nation) a better place to be. The world is already chock-full of corrective opportunities—detection, investigation, arrest, adjudication, and incarceration—all lying in wait for infractions.

Elementary, middle school, and high school students need more than to be told what to do—they need ongoing supportive help in achieving success, and it is our responsibility to support their desire to be successful in school (Di Giulio, 1978). Teachers can promote success in many ways: by simply moving around the classroom, by making eye contact, by walking near students, by making caring gestures like smiling and nodding. And by reminding students—by setting up a system in the classroom not where the teacher spoon-feeds students, but where he or she makes it easy for them to be in charge of their own work. Monitoring student work, for example, can really ensure success. When giving an assignment that's due in one month, we can check student progress in steps: First we have them submit the topic, then later an outline, then a sloppy copy, then the final draft. This process will almost guarantee that all students will get to the final product, having been supported along the way. (Yes, this is for high school students, too.)

A Word on Transitions

With regard to student behavior, transitions are among the most critical times during the school day. By "transitions," I mean when students enter or leave class, usually as a group, at the beginning of the day, the end of the day, and many times in between (changing classes, going to lunch, and so forth). These are the times that the class is at highest risk for disruption, so when they are uneventful and smooth, they serve to help students be successful. In a positive classroom, smooth transition times are very much a part of a teacher's overall supportive interventions, and they are supportive to the entire group.

In general, and for all ages and grade levels, it is best to have transitions consist as much as possible of routine procedures. These will save time and help put students in the right mode for success. Institute any routine you believe is important and educationally sound (for example, the checking of homework, do-now work from the chalkboard, morning meeting, journaling, or group singing). I found it best to ask the more experienced teachers on my floor what they did, and to try out their routines in my classroom. The main purpose for routines is to provide students with a clear and reliable idea of *what to do* (axiom #3), and it ensures they are *doing something* (axiom #2). Avoid at all costs leaving students either with nothing to do or not knowing what to do with each transition—at the very start of the day, at the end of the day, and each time the class is moving from one room or activity to another. As I have said, transitions are high-risk times for disruption. Prepare students and yourself for transitions—don't just let them happen.

Here's an actual example of what to avoid in your students' transitions: One of my student teachers and I were observing a class in a nearby high school. We conferred in the back of the noisy room as the classroom teacher ended his lesson. Ten minutes before the bell, students began lining up on both sides of the exit door to the hall. Looking at my watch, I whispered, "Ten minutes is a long time." My student teacher nodded, seeing that the students—noisy to begin with—had begun shoving each other by the doorway and teasing and poking each other. "Not a good idea," I murmured. The bell finally rang, and as the students tumbled out of the room, the teacher flew to the doorway, stuck his head into the hall, and yelled, "Finish page ninety-one for homework!"

"Not a good move," my student teacher said to me. I agreed, asking him to predict how many students in the next day's class would actually have the homework assignment completed. He predicted that not half of them would, and I had to agree. He added that the teacher should have allowed time for the end-of-class transition, not by having the students crowd around the doorway, but by making sure they knew and understood the assignment before lining up to leave. Plus, we agreed, the teacher should have waited until just before the bell to have the students line up, ensuring that they would not be poking and teasing each other noisily as they waited. Clearer and more direct instructions from the teacher would have helped as well.

Transitions at the end of the day should take similar form. Mr. K, one of the best middle school teachers I ever saw, gave students the gift of time at the end of the day to think about what they needed before lining up to leave. He reviewed the day's high points with the class. Once they lined up, Mr. K went down the line as one would go down a wedding reception line, checking in with each student, shaking his or her hand. Each of them had to tell Mr. K one thing he or she had learned that day. While doing this, Mr. K checked in on certain students who perhaps had been in an argument during lunchtime, or who had been close to a fight, or who had had some other upsetting experience during the day. Mr. K asked directly, "Are you finished with that issue?" "Are you guys okay with each other?" "Do you have something more to work out?" Usually things were fine by that time, but if not, Mr. K took the opportunity to talk with the students who had had an issue. This checking in at the end of the day not only ensured that the upcoming transition (leaving the classroom and school) would be smooth, but it also headed off fights and arguments that might otherwise spill over to the school bus or the school yard. It also helped students be clear about what they needed to do at home for the next day's class meeting. Plus, when they arrived home, students were prepared to give a good, articulate answer to the eternal parental question: "What did you do in school today?"

Attribution Teaching as Supportive Intervention

On a deeper level, supportive intervention means teaching students "who they are"; what their *attributions* are. Mentioned earlier as a preventive in the spiritual dimension, attributions are also a wonderful and affirmative way of supporting students in the managerial dimension. Unlike rewarding students ("No homework for anyone who passes the test!"), persuading students ("You should have passed that test"), or pleading with students ("Why can't you behave yourselves when I'm out of the room?"), teaching students their attributions works wonders. It's similar to *catching students being good*, but differs in that you don't reward them once you catch them. You simply and honestly *reflect* what you see. For example: "You are the first class I've had that knows what to do when finished," or, "Wow. Do you realize I have not once had to ask you to get back to work? Today each of you stayed engaged with your groups the full half hour!" The words must be more than cheerleading; they must be sincere and true. Attributions are even more powerful if they come not only from you, but also from others in the school—the principal, other teachers, staff, and other students.

To make this really powerful, have students reflect on, discuss, and describe their self-attributions, asking, "What do we do well?" Remind students to keep it positive and to keep it plural—speaking of *us* and not *him*, *her*, *you*, or *me*.

This area of the managerial dimension has the greatest potential to make your classroom a winning place, for your students and for yourself. Attribution teaching can be your ticket out of the reward-and-punishment games. Free yourself from worrying about being too positive with your students. If you are sincere and if your students know or suspect that what you say is true, your words will be significant, powerful, and affirming.

CORRECTIVE INTERVENTION: AFTER THE FACT

I wrote earlier that the corrective zone is not the best place to dwell. However, it is a reality of life and teaching that, no matter how preventive and supportive we are, no matter how experienced we may be, because we are dealing with human beings, there will be times every one of us must take corrective action and respond after the fact. While supportive interventions are the joy of teaching, these corrective interventions are the *duty* of teaching, and as such can be unpleasant at times. Often, correctives take the form of *desist strategies*, because we seek to get the student to stop what he or she is doing. Recall that even the most experienced teachers have students who misbehave. But what do those experienced teachers do in response to that misbehavior?

Four things:

Safety. If needed, they protect themselves, other students, and the student who is acting out from the misbehavior. If necessary, they get help—*immediately* if the misbehavior is serious or is continuing.

Continuity. Even if they feel helpless, they fight off paralysis. They keep the teaching-learning process going. They do not involve other students, bring things to a halt, or draw other students away from their tasks. They keep it moving.

Efficiency. They identify and deal with misbehavior easily. This means they do not spend time locating culprits; conducting drama, inquisitions, or trials; seeking witnesses; or making mountains out of molehills. They keep it simple.

Dignity. They never compromise a student's dignity, even if openly insulted or challenged. They know that a teacher's sarcasm and angry words always make matters worse. They avoid making an example of anyone or anyone's misbehavior. They safeguard their own dignity by not providing free entertainment for the class.

Taken together, these principles tell us that when a response to misbehavior is called for, skilled teachers use a stepladder of interventions, starting at the lowest level of force and using the most private, least verbal measures that will work (see figure). Think of the ladder as a scale of intensity of teacher responses to student misbehavior, the lower rungs representing the milder, more private responses and the higher rungs the stronger, more public responses. Just as you always begin to climb a stepladder at the lowest rung, respond to student misbehavior at the lowest possible level. Doctors do not perform surgery if bed rest is all that is needed to restore health. Similarly, if a simple glance can settle a student's minor misbehavior, it is excessive (and exhausting) to publicly yell out the student's name. Keep in mind that you can always go up the ladder to give a more forceful, more public response, but you can never go down the ladder. A less forceful, more private response will not work after a more forceful response has failed. If calling out a student's name does not bring desistance of misbehavior, then simple eye contact will not work, either. That is why it is better to start at the lowest rung.

Of course, not every student misbehavior merits a teacher's response. Of all responses, the one with the lowest level of force is *no response.* Not responding is a valuable tactic for a teacher to use—at suitable times, of course. For example, misbehaviors that do not involve safety, do not distract other students, and are likely to end on their own are best ignored. However, it is not a good practice to ignore student misbehavior simply because you hope it will stop on its own or because you do not know how to respond to it.

Nonverbal Responses

The lowest rung of the ladder represents *not responding at all* to student misbehavior. A student's pencil tapping or staring into space is best ignored, because we know it is likely self-limiting—it will run its course quickly—and it does not intrude on other students' focus. Knowing when to ignore misbehavior takes time and experience and is not simple to learn. New teachers need to be reflective and patient with themselves in this subtle but key area of corrective intervention. My best advice is to start low; try doing nothing (again, provided it is not a matter of safety, is

Ladder of Corrective Teacher Interventions

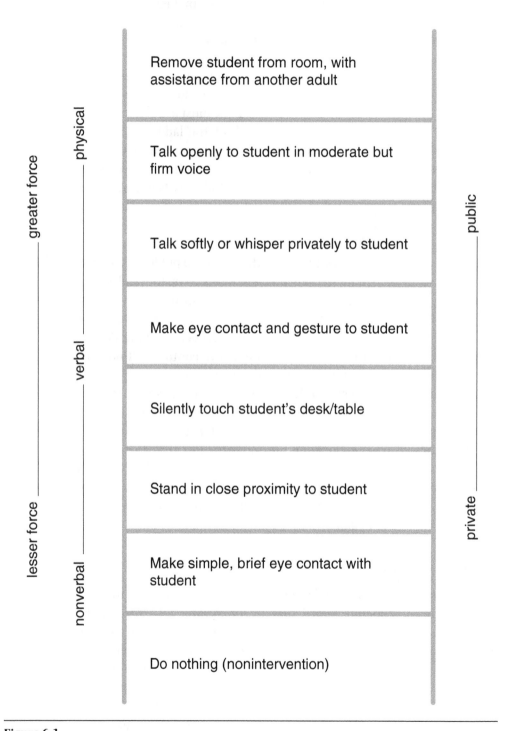

Figure 6.1

not distracting others, and seems temporary), but be ready to go up to the first rung if doing nothing is not working.

Going up one rung is the tacit response of simple eye contact. It is private; he knows and you know, but no one else has a clue. Eye contact works well with students who are off task and are likely to get right back on task. (It's okay, by the way, to smile as you make eye contact at this level.) A fun thing that sometimes happens at this rung is that the student does not notice your eye contact effort right away, but another student seated next to him does. Often, that student will look back at you with an understanding smile, and he or she will usually alert the oblivious student with a gesture toward you. As the rest of the class works on unaware, you have successfully achieved desistance while sharing a grin with two students!

Close-proximity responses are a step higher. Move near the misbehaving student without taking your attention from the other students. This is an especially helpful strategy when you cannot get the culprit's attention, such as when you are waiting for eye contact that does not come. People (students) usually notice movement in their visual field.

At the next rung—signal responses—the teacher makes eye contact with the student, and having secured the student's attention, also uses a gesture such as pointing, shaking his or her head, or frowning. My favorite is holding my index finger vertically and waving it back and forth ("No!") or pointing down ("Get to work!"). Be sure it is private (between you and the student) and not public (for the entire class to see), so there is no humiliation factor.

Signal and closeness responses work well because they are private and personal, seen only by the one or two students for whom they are intended. Furthermore, they are not disruptive to the class, are quiet and efficient, preserve student dignity, enhance your dignity, and are economical, accomplishing much with little teacher exertion. Aim for these, and you will not go home exhausted each night!

Humor Responses

Corrective interventions are usually not fun for teachers, but humor responses can make desist strategies *almost* fun. Humor responses are a special type of teacher talk. They must be used with care, yet they can be very helpful. A simple smile or humorous comment can defuse a potential trouble situation as well as help you lay groundwork for defusing future problems. "Tito" was reported to be a "behavior problem" in another class and was transferred to mine. I placed his desk next to my desk ("therapeutic relocation," I called it). He bonded to me and scrutinized my every move. For instance, Tito noticed when the principal came by to give me my paycheck. With a twinkle in his eye, Tito asked me,

"Payday, Mr. D?" I smiled and put it away. Later, when Tito was off task, trying to bother another student across the classroom, I walked by his desk, pointed to his paper, and whispered, "Someday it's gonna be your payday!" adding, "And remember, Mr. D gets half, right?" He smiled, eating up my attention. But this light humor served a good purpose: It helped Tito go back to his work without my having to reprimand him. "Payday" became our code word for "Get back to work, Tito!"

Public humor helps, too, especially when it opens up discussion. Some students in my class had witnessed the tail end of a lunchtime fistfight in the school yard. After the bedraggled third-grade combatants passed by my classroom's open door as they were escorted to the principal's office, I shook my head and said to my students, "If you're going to box, at least get paid for it!" Julio added, "Yeah, and make sure you got Blue Cross, man!" The students and I laughed, and it served as a springboard for a class discussion. Instead of moralizing about the evils of fighting, and instead of condoning fighting as a way of resolving differences, Julio and I made the point using irony, which resulted in discussion and a teachable moment for our class.

The rest of the dialogue went something like this:

"The real problem, Mr. D, is the other kids. They egg you on."

"Yeah. I got into a fight last week with Hector, and I didn't want to fight him, but everybody was making me."

"'Making you'? Can somebody 'make' you fight?"

"Sure. Easy. They make you feel small if you don't. They call you 'chicken.'"

"What can you do if you don't want to fight? Kaitlin?"

"You can stay away from bad kids . . ."

"You can stay away from Hector!"

"Mr. D, do you know what else you can do? Don't make other kids fight!"

"What do you mean by that, Jacob?"

"You know, when you're near the kids who want to fight, don't let other people make the kids fight."

"Isn't that hard to do? What do you think, Jorge?"

"Yes . . . uh, no, it's not hard. You just tell them to back off. And if that doesn't work you move between the two kids. Kids really don't want to fight. But they just don't want to look cheap by backing off. If you help them, there won't be a fight."

"That sounds good to me. What else can you do? Tyler?"

Sarcasm and ridicule have no place in any classroom, and they should never be confused with genuine humor. Another caution: Humor responses must not be used in situations that are dangerous or threaten to get out of hand. At such times, humor can send the wrong message to a student. However, at the right moment, humor responses can be an extremely valuable way to convey a message while preserving human dignity. They can be the best type of kind talk within a classroom.

Verbal Responses

Verbal responses are always public, and as such they lose the special power that private, nonverbal responses carry. Verbal responses are usually used for students who do not respond to nonverbal responses, and they are also used when you must intervene more quickly or more forcefully, such as when misbehavior is disruptive to other students. Do not use humor in these situations. To be effective, verbal interventions must be as unambiguous as possible.

At the lowest level of verbal response, the teacher speaks privately, directly to the student but out of earshot of anyone else. It can be a whisper ("Sam, this needs to be completed!") combined with a gesture, or it can be a private conference at the student's or teacher's desk. Speak softly—so it does not involve others—but firmly. Be sure the student is listening, even if he or she is looking down. Do not speak if the student is fooling with another or is distracted by something or someone else. Be patient. Speaking privately but clearly, remind the student of the standard expected in your classroom.

The next higher level of verbal response is public and directed at an individual. It is spoken loud enough for most or all others to hear. Many teachers erroneously start off at this level, even for misbehavior that would be best handled at a lower level ("Ashley, it's always such a mess by your desk! Pick up those papers now!"). What the teacher has done is waste his energy and attack Ashley's dignity, even if she gamely smiles at those around her. Worst of all, the teacher has too quickly upped the ante. By going public, the teacher now has little maneuvering room for more serious misbehaviors (you can't go down a rung, only up). Had he simply gotten Ashley's attention while the class did their work, he could have pointed at the paper on the floor and silently mouthed the word "please" or "paper." It works.

If you must make public verbal responses, make them as clear and as businesslike as possible.

Verbal responses are often directed to the entire class. Because this is what a teacher normally does in the act of teaching, great care must be taken to use an appropriate tone of voice. Screaming is never effective.

Addressing the entire class in a serious, calm voice can help convey your dissatisfaction, for example, with a high classroom noise level. (My students listened best when I *whispered*. Even as a principal standing in the middle of the lunchroom, I began talking in a normal voice, and within seconds students were quietly attending to my words. There was no need for bells, whistles, or threats.) It is in these cases that preventing works better than reacting: Doing something before the fact of group misbehavior is far more effective than trying to fix things after the fact. In the case of a high group noise level, the teacher's response is best expressed preventively. In a calm, serious voice (and with all eyes on her), the teacher says, "The noise level is high. Remember our discussion about how a lot of noise makes it hard to think? Let's give it another try."

Save your public voice for teaching, and use it more for preventing and supporting than correcting.

Physical Responses

"Getting physical" represents the highest rung on the ladder, and should be used rarely. Never touch a student. Well, almost never. Tapping a student on the shoulder, shaking a student's hand, or holding a young child's hand may be acceptable. Avoid initiating any greater physical contact (hugging, picking up kids, horsey rides, etc.). This is true for all teachers, but especially for male teachers (generally the public is more uneasy about male teachers expressing physical affection than it is about female teachers doing so). Teachers are at risk of being accused of child abuse if an innocent hug is misconstrued. Elementary students are young and incapable of knowing what they are getting into when they receive affectionate physical contact from an unrelated adult. In general, it is safest for all teachers—male or female—to avoid all but the most superficial physical contact with students, even those in high school.

Except when it comes to restraining a student who is a danger to himself, herself, or others, teachers must avoid forceful physical contact. In my opinion, corporal punishment serves no constructive purpose and only makes matters worse. It teaches the wrong thing—that aggression solves problems. Plus, once you resort to corporal punishment, you have to keep using it over the course of the school year to maintain compliance (and being beaten doesn't necessarily assure compliance). Twenty-two states still have laws permitting corporal punishment, but even within those states are many school districts that have outlawed it. Regardless of the legality or illegality of corporal punishment, I say never strike a student, no matter how horrid his or her behavior. After 35 years as an educator and 30 years as a parent and grandparent, I have never seen or heard of one beneficial outcome resulting from an adult hitting a child or adolescent, even when "it's for the child's own good." If the truth must be told, it never is.

Crisis Time: Reacting to More Serious Problem Behaviors

At some point you may be faced with serious student misbehavior, and for this, as for anything else in teaching, it pays to plan ahead. Talk with teachers from past years. Ask them what worked with Janelle, what did not work with Justin. Ahead of time, plan how you will react to misbehavior. What action will you take? What consequences will be carried out?

Here are several response strategies I have collected from experienced teachers who have been faced with relatively serious student misbehavior. I have used many of these strategies myself with good results. Unless otherwise qualified, they are useful at all levels: elementary, middle school, and high school.

- ✓ **Talking to the student.** Use "I" messages, such as, "I am disappointed by [specify student's misbehavior]. I cannot allow it to continue." This is the next step when a student's misbehavior has not responded to the supportive strategies described above. This is useful when the student can—will be allowed to and will be able to—return to work.

- ✗ DO NOT USE: When the student is enraged or seems likely to openly shrug off or otherwise reject your verbal disapproval.

- ✓ **Withholding classroom privileges** (special events, free time or recess time, desirable tasks). This is useful when the student already knows the limits and what the result or consequence of disregarding that limit will be. Limits are boundaries, and they must be clear, concise, and concrete. As discussed earlier, we teach limits best by discussion, by talking to and with our students. When the limit is disregarded and the student is given a supportive reminder that does not work, the result of that violation—the consequence—is loss of a classroom privilege.

- ✗ DO NOT USE: If the consequence of limit violation has not been discussed by and made clear to the entire class. Do not use it as a punishment or in a spiteful way. If you do, you are likely to incur a hostile response: "I didn't want to go to recess *anyway!*"

✓ **Excluding the student from class.** This is a powerful consequence, especially when used in a positive classroom where students want to stay. Used sparingly, it can be very effective. However, exclusion can create resentment, and excluding a student removes an opportunity he or she may have had to learn suitable classroom behavior. As with all consequences, students must know (through prior class discussion on basic understandings and limits) the limit that was disregarded, the amount of time to be spent in exclusion, and what they are expected to do during that time.

✗ DO NOT USE: If the student has not had a chance to be part of the class discussion or sees exclusion as a reward, or if there is no safe, secure, and supervised place for the student to spend his or her exile. Also, be aware that exclusion is too often used in many high schools, and sometimes so overused that students may not even regard it as a corrective: "Leave? Gladly!"

✓ **Reflective activities.** These ask the student to think about what took place, and how he or she might have acted differently. For example, have the student write about his or her misbehavior. Reflective writing is useful for students who are in older elementary grades, middle school, and high school, enhancing self-monitoring and among the best noncoercive tools a teacher can use to promote self-discipline.

✗ DO NOT USE: With young children.

✓ **Prosocial detention.** Detention (staying after school) can be a really positive learning experience if it gives a student one-to-one time with the teacher. During this time, students can open up and let go of the defensiveness (and cheekiness) that they display in front of an audience. Lunchtime is another possible opportunity for this. A detention in which a student is isolated and sits out an hour or two is not productive; it is a waste of time and sows seeds of resentment.

✗ DO NOT USE: Without prior discussion of basic understandings and limits. Do not use without clear communication with the student's parent beforehand. Be clear on how and when the student will get home from school. Detention is another consequence that is too often used in many high schools. If this is the case at your school, try to explore other options with colleagues.

✓ **Contacting parents.** This is more than important; it is necessary. Even if you do not expect there is much the parents can do to remedy their child's misbehavior, parental awareness of the problem and their wish to cooperate are vital to your management plan. Involve parents early, and be prepared to outline your ideas. They will look to you for specific action, because they probably already know all too well about their child's misbehavior.

✗ DO NOT USE: Generally, there is no circumstance when parental involvement is to be avoided. Caution is necessary with parents who may abuse their children in reaction to your words. Never ask parents to punish children for school misbehavior. Indeed, help parents see that you are on top of the situation and are exploring options with them.

✓ **Creating a daily report card.** This is helpful for chronic or recurring misbehavior in a positive classroom. It offers feedback, promotes reflection, and when used appropriately, encourages the student to monitor his or her own behavior. Here is one way to construct a daily report card: Draw rows and columns on a piece of paper. List one date per box down the first column. Each day, send the card home with your signature to the right of the day's date box. In the next box to the right, write briefly how well the student did at the behavior you are focusing on. The next box to the right is for the student's signature, and the last box is for the parent's signature. Have the student initial it, take it home, and bring it back the next morning with the parent's signature. If you wish, add another column for the parent's comments. Do this for a limited time; a week to 10 days may be sufficient. Parental signatures may be omitted when you use this card with high school students.

✗ DO NOT USE: Again, there are few circumstances when parental involvement is to be avoided. Be sure you communicate with the parent before beginning the daily report card.

✓ **Self-instruction strategies.** These strategies, which have been used with success by many teachers, involve students' use of specific, planned responses to situations that seem to accompany misbehavior. Typically, students use self-instruction strategies as substitutes for their unacceptable behaviors. For example, a student who has thrown food in the lunchroom at the instigation of other students would be taught a specific strategy to use at the time of instigation. It could be as simple as getting up to use the bathroom or telling the instigators, "I'm too hungry right now," or, "I don't have to do what you say." Self-instruction strategies are useful with both older and younger students.

✗ DO NOT USE: With students who have little or no insight into their own behavior. Talk to the student first; get an idea of how much insight he or she possesses.

✓ **Contracts.** For older students, contracts can be effectively used for a variety of behaviors, ranging from class participation (waiting for a turn to speak, raising a hand) to academic production (turning in work, completing homework). The teacher and student (and sometimes the parent as well) make up a contract. It should be as specific as possible, outlining acceptable behavior and what credit the student will earn or get as a result of this behavior. The contract should have a time limit. If the time is too long (weeks or months), some students will have difficulty seeing the agreement through. Make the time just long enough to allow the student to be successful in the new behavior.

✗ DO NOT USE: To negotiate basic understandings or quibble about limits. Beware of such contracts as, "If I don't hit nobody for a week, I get no homework, okay?" Not hitting others is a nonnegotiable standard of behavior among human beings.

✓ **Involving the principal.** This is important for serious misbehavior. The principal can be an important support person, and even if not, he or she should be apprised early on of instances of misbehavior. However, avoid using the principal as an enforcer.

✗ DO NOT USE: The principal's office routinely, or for anything less than a serious issue. Your leadership will be compromised (undermined) if you regularly rely on the principal (or anyone else) to handle your classroom management.

Even More Serious Misbehavior

You may be faced with the necessity to address the tougher stuff. At these times, the main idea is to act with your head, not your emotions.

Taking these situations personally keeps you from being the only rational, cool head present. Remain calm and collected.

✓ **Dealing with fighting.** The highest level of corrective physical response comes with breaking up a fight, or defending yourself or another student from a student's physical attack. When attempting to break up a fight, if your voice does not separate the fighters, stepping between children may be the only choice you have to prevent student injury. With adolescents, beware of physically intervening if you are physically smaller or weaker. In that case, send for help, and continue to direct your voice—strong and clear without screaming—at the fighters. If circumstances permit, get uninvolved students out of the area. Removing an audience can be very helpful. If you are yourself the object of attack, you certainly have the right to protect yourself. However, do so without excessive force, such as angrily pummeling a student into submission. In anticipation of situations such as these, it is best to set up a plan with a nearby colleague in which he or she will come to your assistance. As part of this plan, you might designate a trusted, reliable student to automatically fetch Mr. Smith next door (or the principal) if you are incapacitated or your efforts are ineffective.

✓ **Dealing with threats of assault.** If threatened by a student with a gun, knife, or other weapon, do not attempt to physically remove the weapon. Nor should you attempt to overpower the student or direct another student to intervene. Use your voice—again, strong and clear without screaming—and clearly tell the student what you want him or her to do. Make no fast or sudden movements. Do not make threats. Repeat your verbal directions. Be a broken record.

Be sure that you actually are being threatened with assault. (Hearing a rumor that a student may have a knife or a gun means you should act, but it does not necessarily mean you act as if under siege or assault.) If you hear that a student has a weapon (or even if you see the outline of what looks like a weapon in a student's clothing), do not rush to immediately confiscate the weapon. After sending for help (principal, counselor, other designated adult), keep the student within sight while you calmly repeat your instruction to him. No screaming, no fast moves, no strong feelings—just a calm-sounding broken record, telling the student what you want him or her to do, again and again and again if needed.

It is a good idea to set up a plan before such an incident happens. Some high schools as a matter of policy have established a procedure for the office (called "Code Red" or something similar), or a means by which police are summoned expeditiously and efficiently without enraging an armed or threatening student. If your school has no plan in place, bring this subject up at a staff meeting. With your colleagues and administration, establish a crisis intervention plan. Some schools include intervention under the term *postvention*: how the school staff will react to an unexpected, difficult incident. Check the school district's policy manual, and talk to experienced staff and administration to learn if postvention procedures are already established and, if so, what they are. (A helpful reference for handling student violence and fighting is presented in Charles Wolfgang's *Solving Discipline and Classroom Management Problems* [2004].)

In conclusion, if you are faced with serious misbehavior that is more than disruptive and potentially harmful:

✓ Never attempt to impose consequences upon a student who is armed or a student who is distraught, visibly angry, or fresh from the fray.

✓ Never strike a student. Even if you are openly challenged ("Go ahead, hit me!"), you will not solve a thing by hitting students. You will not lose face by refusing the student's challenge to fight, because keeping a cool head at those times is the real proof of your strength. "I don't need to hit you, Andrew," says more about your character and professionalism than giving in. You cannot teach placid behavior to your students if you model hostile behavior toward them or other students.

✓ Never attempt to use words alone when an unarmed student is out of control and likely to harm himself, herself, or another. In these most serious cases, physically restrain and/or remove the student from the classroom. Do not strike or hurt a student in the process of restraining or removal. Reassure the student—so others hear as well as the student—that you do not hurt students and that you do not allow students to hurt you. If you are overmatched in size or bulk or both, get help immediately from another adult.

It pays to repeat: Thinking about what to do before something happens helps. All teachers must react to unplanned events. Yet even the best and most skillful teacher *reactions* are never as effective as teacher *actions*. Preventing and supporting before the fact are much better than reacting and correcting after the fact. Researcher and educator Pedro Noguera sums it up quite well:

> The urban schools that I know that feel safe to those who spend their time there don't have metal detectors or armed security guards, and their principals don't carry baseball bats. What these schools do have is a strong sense of community and collective responsibility. Such schools are seen by students as sacred territory, too special to be spoiled by crime and violence, and too important to risk one's being excluded. Such schools are few, but their existence serves as tangible proof that there are alternatives to chaotic schools plagued by violence. (1995, p. 206)

PART III

Blueprints
for Success

Preparing
Your Classroom

Although we have all seen good teaching, few of us have seen the preparation that goes into it. Good teachers are good because they work at it, not only as they are teaching, but also before—and after—they walk into the classroom. Good teachers know that being prepared is indispensable: Winging it doesn't work, and it cheats students. Time is wasted when a teacher flounders around trying to decide what to do next.

Because we seldom see what a teacher does behind the scenes, I designed this blueprint to give an X-ray of the preparation teachers do to create positive classrooms. As a blueprint, it is not a complete representation of the finished product, but a checklist of the most essential tasks from each dimension.

There are three checklists, one each for early, later, and first-day preparation. Early preparation tasks are best begun at least a month or so before the start of teaching (perhaps during summer break); later preparation tasks should be attended to at least a week before beginning instruction. The third and final checklist is for the first day of school. Look over that checklist a couple of days before the school year begins, and bring it to school the first day as a helpful reminder.

A few tasks in early preparation (Checklist I) may seem obvious to the more experienced teacher, but many could be just as easily overlooked. For instance, even the most experienced of teachers must become familiar with school policies that relate to student health and safety. For every teacher, old or new, the guiding principle behind preparation is to set up a safe, educationally sound environment and program for students—a positive classroom—that will incubate student success.

In the checklists below, review each task, then check the thumbs-up "All set" box (👍) on the left when you have taken care of the task or have decided what to do about it, or if it does not apply. Now you can see at a glance the items still needing your attention.

Check the "Not yet" box (✋) next to all tasks that need follow-up, that you are not yet clear about, or that need to be taken care of before school starts.

Although the first checklist should optimally be reviewed a month or so before school starts, experienced teachers can use it midstream to make sure nothing has been overlooked. A Notes section is provided at the end of each checklist for you to record items that require follow-up.

CHECKLIST I: PREPARATION— A MONTH BEFORE INSTRUCTION

Spiritual Dimension

👍   ✋

☐   ☐   Visit the school when it is not in session. Visit your classroom-to-be. Sit in the space you'll occupy as a teacher. Sit in the space your students will occupy. How does it feel to you?

☐   ☐   Think about what would start things off in a great way on the very first day of school. What might you do to make that first day and first week special?

☐   ☐   Think back: What made you want to go to school? What made you feel you belonged there? What made you feel safe there?

☐   ☐   What successes can your students experience the first day? The first week? Brainstorm a list of activities students can do early on that will provide them with success.

☐   ☐   Look around your classroom. Is there anything about it that doesn't feel right? Is it a place you'd like to spend many hours each day? If not, what can you do about it before school starts?

☐   ☐   Mentally frame the upcoming school year as *the moment you've been waiting for.* What are some exciting things that could take place? What are some activities your students might enjoy? What special events can you create for the school year? How can this school year be the moment *they've* been waiting for?

Notes:

_____

_____

_____

_____

_____

_____

_____

_____

_____

_____

_____

_____

_____

_____

_____

Physical Dimension

☝ ✋

☐ ☐ Whenever you visit the school, bring your to-do list. At an early visit, introduce yourself to the school secretary, the principal, neighboring teachers, and the school's custodian. These people will be very important to your success as a teacher.

☐ ☐ Get keys—to the school, your classroom, and any closets and file cabinets.

☐ ☐ Go to your classroom or teaching area. Try the keys to the classroom door, closets, and file cabinets. As you enter your room-to-be, get a feel for the room. Is it hospitable? Gloomy?

☐ ☐ Count desks and chairs and tables—have you enough for each student? Do not start the term without a place for each student to sit, to work, to contemplate, to be sociable.

☐ ☐ Determine if the size of student desks, tables, and chairs is appropriate for your students' age group. For example, if you will be teaching fifth grade, be sure you have not been stuck with surplus second-graders' desks and kindergarten-size chairs. No matter what grade you will teach, always keep a few larger desks and chairs on hand for heavier or taller students. If you are not sure what size your furniture should be, a little too large is better than a little too small. (Check the legs of the desks and chairs—the height of some can easily be adjusted with a Phillips-head screwdriver.)

☐ ☐ Arrange the desks or tables and chairs in any orderly pattern. You can rearrange them before school begins.

☐ ☐ Examine the furniture, both yours and your students'—file cabinets, desks, tables, chairs, cubbies, bookcases. With your hand, rock each desk and chair back and forth. It should sit foursquare. Chairs or desks that rock can be extremely distracting to students, so put taking care of them on your to-do list, or mark them with a piece of colored cloth tape for the school custodian to attend to. Look over the other furniture, too. Hold your hand on each piece and gently rock it back and forth. Is anything broken? Make sure that all bookcases and tall furniture are anchored. Students have been known to climb classroom furniture with deadly results.

☐ ☐ Check the closets. Are there closets for supplies? Is there a closet for your things? A closet for student coats and hats? Could someone get locked in or out by mistake?

☐ ☐ Try all the windows. Do they work? Are any of them broken? Are they in need of cleaning? Does each of the shades work?

☐ ☐ Turn off the lights—is there much natural light? Turn on the lights—how adequate is the lighting? (If the room is cold, fluorescent lights will be dimmer than usual, or they may not work at all. Try them again when the room is warmer.)

☐ ☐ Check out the heating/cooling system. Is there a thermostat or temperature sensor in the classroom? Does it work? (Open a window for a brief time to kick it on.)

☐ ☐ Look for odors. Does the room smell bad? If so, find out why.

☐ ☐ Examine the room for safety. Are there any obvious unsafe items such as cracked or broken glass, cracks in the floor or walls, exposed insulation, wires that are bare or pullable, jutting nails, or clothing hooks at the students' or teacher's eye level? Find out if the school is safe from asbestos hazards. Is there any loose, friable insulation on pipes or walls? Even if it contains no asbestos, friable insulation is not acceptable. Look up: Is the ceiling in good shape? Are there cracks or bulges? Some schools (especially those in the inner city) are more than 100 years old. You may be the first person in many years who has examined conditions in the classroom!

☐ ☐ Locate the exits. Are there at least two classroom exits? (Older buildings might have only one exit.) Inspect the locks on the doors: Could you or your students accidentally get locked in? Locked out?

☐ ☐ Turn on all classroom computers and audiovisual equipment. Do they work? Move unusable and obsolete hardware and software out of your room.

☐ ☐ Walk through the school. Locate the nearest exit for your classroom. Find your way to the lunchroom, gym, library, office, nurse.

☐ ☐ Go outside and look over the place your students will spend recess. Are there any potential trouble spots (trees, climbing structures, etc.)? Places to hide out of sight of the adult in charge? Where will students have recess on rainy days?

☐ ☐ Check your to-do list. Request any needed maintenance or repair *today*. (Do not wait until the week before school starts!)

☐ ☐ P.S. Do you have a place to park your car?

Notes:

_____

_____

_____

_____

_____

_____

_____

_____

_____

_____

_____

_____

_____

Instructional Dimension

👍   🖐

☐   ☐   From the school secretary or principal, get a copy of the parent and student handbooks, and read them over. Check anything you do not understand or agree with, and discuss it with the principal.

☐   ☐   Get other documents such as state standards, teacher/student schedules, attendance/absence procedures, bathroom/out-of-room guidelines, procedures for emergencies or unexpected school closings (owing to inclement weather, for example), and school rules.

☐   ☐   Find out how many students will be in your class.

☐   ☐   Get a plan book, an attendance book, and a grade book. (Before you buy them, ask if the school provides them.) Even if your school administrator will not check teachers' plan books, be sure to get one anyway, and use it.

☐   ☐   Obtain supplies, at least enough to see you through the first month or so. Essentials include chalk/dry markers, chalkboard/dry board erasers, pencils, wastebasket, tape, stapler, green pens/pencils for marking and grading, and paper. Are there any other supplies you will need?

☐   ☐   Bring home copies of student textbooks and materials so you may familiarize yourself with each.

☐   ☐   Find out what you are supposed to teach. Locate the curriculum for the school and look it over. Think about how it applies to you and to your students. Using the curriculum and other resources, divide the year into units (big chunks of instruction). If you are an elementary teacher, review one subject at a time. (You can integrate content areas and differentiate instruction later.) For example, with fourth-grade math, divide the year into teaching units on basic operations, geometry, problem solving, measurement, and fractions.

Notes:

_____

_____

_____

_____

_____

_____

_____

_____

_____

_____

_____

_____

_____

_____

Managerial Dimension

👍 🖐

☐ ☐ From the school secretary or principal, obtain a copy of the policy manual printed by the board of education or school district. You may not think it relevant, but if there is an accident or a lawsuit, the court will look at the school district's policy on the issue. Schools have policies on a variety of matters that affect your job, like book selection, corporal punishment, homework amounts, retention and promotion, teacher dress, holiday gift giving, sexual harassment, and so forth. In the event of a question or problem, your ignorance of school policy will not save you. Read the policy manual. If you question or disagree with a policy, discuss it with the principal or lead teacher.

☐ ☐ Read school policies. Pay special attention to policies in areas such as:

   – How to deal with student illness or injury.

   – What to do with students at risk because of health problems (hemophilia, HIV/AIDS, etc.). Review at-risk students with a nurse, school psychologist, or counselor. Have a clear idea of what course of action to take in the event of an emergency (such as the procedure for obtaining 911 assistance).

   – How to report suspected child maltreatment—physical, emotional, or sexual abuse—and neglect. To whom should you report it?

   – How and with whom to share suspicions of student alcohol or drug abuse, or of possession of firearms or other weapons.

   – How to handle prescription medicines sent in by parents.

☐ ☐ Write out a list of important school procedures. Specifically, learn procedures that apply to field trips, emergencies, fire drills, exits to use for lunch and dismissal, playground/recess areas, and the location of equipment. Tape the list to the back of your plan book, and use a highlighting marker to mark crucial facts. Even if you learn these procedures quickly, leave the list taped there. When you are absent, a substitute teacher will need that information.

☐ ☐ Pick out a mentor or buddy teacher in your school. Is there a grade leader (or any other experienced teacher) with whom you can talk and ask questions as they arise? She or he will be a very great advantage to you, whether you are a beginning or a veteran teacher.

☐ ☐ Locate your students' permanent records. There should be a folder for each student that contains health and academic records. Sometimes there are social records as well. Have extra folders handy to store temporary records for new students who arrive during the school year.

☐ ☐ Skim the student records. Look for special-needs students, including those with disabilities, those who are gifted/talented, those with a history of health or behavior problems, and those needing special arrangements because of religion. Check for students whose parents have custody arrangements stipulating who may—and may not—pick up or otherwise remove a student from school.

☐ ☐ Write all student names in your attendance book. Enter flags for the special-needs students and for those with custody, behavior, or health problems. To preserve confidentiality, make a mark in the column next to the name and be sure to provide an interpretive key for yourself (and for the substitute teacher).

☐ ☐ Count names. How many students will you have in all, who will need supplies, books, and materials? Round your number up to the next five, just to be safe. For example, if 21 students are scheduled to be in your class, use 25 as your working number, to allow for the inevitable new students who enroll the first day of school. Even if you have a set list of students, round the number up. (No teacher ever winds up with fewer students. Somehow—and I don't know how this is mathematically possible—every teacher gets more students after the first day of school!)

☐ ☐ Store all books and materials you will not need. Put them away—do not use valuable classroom shelf space for long-term storage. Clutter can be ugly, and dangerous.

☐ ☐ Compile warm-up activities you will use. Include age-appropriate activities for breaking the ice.

☐ ☐ For each student, set up a folder in an empty file drawer or file box where you will store selected samples of his or her work. Think ahead to parent conferences.

☐ ☐ Start thinking about the type of classroom climate you would like to create. (Don't dismiss your ideas as too idealistic!) Review Abraham Maslow's (1970) needs hierarchy. Low-level deficit needs (food, safety, acceptance, etc.) must be satisfied before higher-level growth needs can be met.

☐ ☐ Write out several goals related to student health and well-being. For instance, how will you help your students feel safe in your classroom? Think about psychological safety—will you take a strong stand against bullying or other rude behavior students may direct against each other? What basic understandings will you seek to establish?

☐ ☐ How might you build classroom spirit? A sense of symbolic identification, where students share ownership of and identify with the classroom?

☐ ☐ Your credibility as a teacher will spell the difference between success and failure—it is that vital. There are many ways that you can establish and strengthen your credibility in students' eyes. What might some of those ways be?

Notes:

_____

_____

_____

_____

_____

_____

_____

_____

_____

_____

_____

_____

_____

CHECKLIST II: PREPARATION—2 WEEKS BEFORE TEACHING

Spiritual Dimension

☐ ☐ Check your original brainstormed list of success-related ideas. Revise/update as needed.

☐ ☐ Think about how you will reach out to parents. You want them to have a great start, too. Will you send home an introduction letter? Will you schedule parent-teacher meetings? Will you telephone parents to introduce yourself? Good advice: Introduce yourself to, meet, and/or telephone parents *before* you must do so.

☐ ☐ Think about decorations, and how they can reflect a welcoming sense. Think about leaving plenty of blank spaces to be filled with your students' works (remember: symbolic identification).

☐ ☐ Put together a tentative list of exciting things the class can do this year, including hosting guest speakers, field trips, parties, exhibitions of student work, "parents' day" (or "grandparents' day"), and collaborative ventures with other teachers.

☐ ☐ Decide on ways you can be comfortable describing to your students their attributions.

☐ ☐ How might you set it up so students can describe *their own* perceptions of their attributions?

☐ ☐ Corny, but here goes: How you can show your students you love and respect them?

Physical Dimension

👍 ✋

☐ ☐ Arrange desks and furniture for the first day of school. Decide how you want them placed based on your instructional style and plans. (If you are still not sure, arrange them in rectangular cluster groups of four to six desks.)

☐ ☐ Figure out lines of sight in your room in the following way: Stand near your desk. Walk to the chalkboard. Walk to the windows, then to the exit doorway. At each point, will you be able to see each student without obstruction? Conversely, will each student be able to see you?

☐ ☐ Picture students moving in the room. Will they move smoothly? Are there bottleneck points where students will bump into one another?

☐ ☐ Follow up on requests for repair or replacement of equipment.

☐ ☐ For elementary schools, check out recess equipment. What equipment will students use during recess? Where is equipment stored?

☐ ☐ Double-check: Are there any potentially dangerous conditions?

☐ ☐ Review emergency procedures: Are they clear? Are they written down?

☐ ☐ Decorate. Make the room cheery and inviting. Bare or shabby bulletin boards are a desolate sight! Because you do not yet have student work to display, it is better to use store-bought decorations and to hang objects and pictures that relate to work you will be covering first than it is to have bare bulletin boards and walls.

☐ ☐ Make sure there is some wall or bulletin board space left vacant, ready for displaying your students' best works.

Instructional Dimension

👍 ✋

☐ ☐ Prepare materials for the first day. For kindergarten through Grade 2, prepare name tags, cards, or headbands made of strips of heavy paper.

☐ ☐ Look through your old portfolios or file folders. What can you use this school year for your classroom and students? Find those wonderful lesson plans/unit plans you wrote for student teaching and include them in your teaching plan for this school year.

☐ ☐ Make copies of your class roster. On a sheet of paper, list your students' names on the left in alphabetical order, then duplicate the list. You can use copies to keep track of assignments, trip money, permission slips, and just about anything else.

☐ ☐ Introduce yourself to educational aides or assistants with whom you'll be working. Set up a way for you to meet regularly, especially if there is a student's IEP (individual education plan) involved.

Review your instructional expectations and make critical decisions:

☐ ☐ How will students be expected to participate?

☐ ☐ How much time will your students spend in solo learning and in cooperative learning? Try the "thirds" system—one third of the time students work alone; one third of the time they work with a partner; one third of the time they work as part of a group.

☐ ☐ When a student needs help to complete seat work, what should he or she do to secure assistance? Ask a buddy? Ask the teacher? Call out? Raise a hand? Display an individual HELP, PLEASE card or red flag?

☐ ☐ Will you expect students to raise their hands before being recognized? Will you allow students to not raise their hands? What should they do?

☐ ☐ What should students do when their work is completed? How is work to be submitted? (When you ask? Automatically placed in their folder? Placed in your "In" basket?)

☐ ☐ What will students who have finished do while others are still working? Work on an ongoing project? Go to a special interest/learning center? Post a chart of activities so you can point to it when a student says, "I'm done. What should I do now?"

☐ ☐ If some students have not finished their work when others have, when should the students who haven't finished complete their work? Should they do it for homework? Finish it during recess? Finish it during any free time during the day?

☐ ☐ Will you accept late work? If yes, how late? If not, why not? Under what circumstances will you accept it?

☐ ☐ Will you assign homework each night? What will you do with homework the next day? Collect it? Have students check it? What if it is not done at all?

☐ ☐ When will your students do seat work? This is work students do at their desks, typically alone. Seat work usually consists of work assigned after a lesson for practicing a newly learned skill. Sometimes it involves drill. Seat work must be done in a quiet area. Do not plan instruction or high activity when students are doing seat work.

☐ ☐ How often will you give tests? What other evaluation techniques will you use? Conferencing? Performance tests? Projects? Authentic assessments?

Managerial Dimension

👍 ✋

☐ ☐ Decide how students will get supplies. Individually? By group?

☐ ☐ Review the school policy on absence. Are notes required?

☐ ☐ Review the school policy on lateness. What will you expect of students who enter late? Will you expect them to catch up? Work with a buddy? Jump right in?

☐ ☐ Write down school procedures regarding playground time, recess, and assemblies. What will your role and your class's roles be in these events?

☐ ☐ Decide how you will handle record keeping (report cards, grade book, progress reports, communicating results to students and parents).

☐ ☐ For the elementary grades, decide on classroom jobs. Which jobs need to be done? How will you parcel them out? Who will do them? At what time or period during the day? Specific jobs might include watering plants, cleaning certain spaces, being an office monitor, distributing or collecting supplies, handing out snacks, or marking the calendar.

☐ ☐ Decide how you will handle seating. Once your students enter the classroom, how will they know where to sit? Will you assign seats? May they choose seats?

Make sure you know how your students will move around the school:

☐ ☐ Where will you meet your students each day? (Will they come to the room, or do teachers or aides go to meet them?)

☐ ☐ Where will they eat lunch?

☐ ☐ Where does recess occur? What about when the weather is inclement? Who supervises recess?

☐ ☐ Where and when will their special classes (music, art, etc.) meet?

Plan for individual student movement in and out of the classroom:

☐ ☐ Does the school require a hall pass? A sign-out book?

☐ ☐ How will students get to the rest room? Ask your permission each time? Just leave quietly? Take a partner? Sign out?

Plan for group movement in and out of the classroom:

☐ ☐ Will your students line up? If so, by what criteria? By height? By table? By row? By group? By "Boys in one line, girls in another"? Assigned spots in line, or stand where you want?

☐ ☐ What are the procedures involved in preparing for lunch, special periods, activities, fire drills, going home, and recess?

☐ ☐ What are the procedures for students entering the room at the start of the day, after an activity or recess, after lunch, and after a fire drill?

☐ ☐ What are dismissal routines? Movement within the school? Order of classes in dismissal?

☐ ☐ What is the routine for sharpening pencils? For using the bathroom? Using the wastebasket? Going to the learning center? Working in cooperative groups?

Notes:

_____

_____

_____

_____

_____

_____

_____

_____

_____

_____

_____

_____

_____

_____

CHECKLIST III: FIRST-DAY PREPARATION

If you have been thorough in covering tasks in Checklists I and II, completing this last checklist should be pleasant, if not easy. The tasks in this section are mostly physical and managerial. You will need to fill in the instructional details for your first day, such as content (what lesson you will teach) and specifics that apply only to your school and teaching situation. Conditions for addressing the spiritual dimension should already be in place, ready for the students to enter.

👍 ✋

☐ ☐ Print your name on the board: "Ms. Brooks" (for upper grades, cursive is fine). Identify the class: "Class 2–1." Print legibly, because students will model your writing.

☐ ☐ With elementary students, practice entering the classroom. If there is disorder upon entry, have students practice entering again: First line up the class to exit, then give a signal to exit: "Stop at the first bulletin board in the hall. About-face." Have students reenter the classroom.

☐ ☐ Orient students to the classroom, teacher, teacher's name, and one another. Will you have the students identify themselves?

☐ ☐ Discuss expectations—theirs, yours, and both of yours together. Be clear on nonnegotiables, but don't present them in a dire or harsh way.

☐ ☐ Continue orientation. Where do students hang their coats/clothing? Store their personal books and book bags? Lunches? Snacks?

☐ ☐ Discuss basic student jobs. Who does what? When do they do it? Where do they do it? How will they be selected for these jobs?

☐ ☐ Point out what each student's private space (desk or table) is. Point out what your private space is.

☐ ☐ Clearly set out key limits, like, "Listen quietly while others speak." Be sure to establish these limits now, so that you can have productive discussions of basic understandings later on! If you have chaos, interruption, and disorder during this very first discussion, stop. (It will not get better the second day; it will only get worse.) Start over—today—clearly restating the limits. If you must, start over again. Hard work and persistence on your part now will pay off for the rest of the school year.

☐ ☐ Once key limits are clear, lead a brief practice discussion, perhaps an extension of the earlier instruction on "Listen while others speak" For older grades, the topic can be related to an upcoming content area issue.

☐ ☐ Start to build a class ethic. For example, describe how the class is like a family. Elicit from students what qualities you all must exhibit to succeed—sharing, patience, consideration for others, helping others when you can, and so forth. This idea of a shared ethic is particularly valuable in high school classrooms.

☐ ☐ Teach a lesson the first morning, something that will help students get used to their new teacher and the class.

☐ ☐ Establish the practice of students writing down their homework assignments.

☐ ☐ Have students do at least one thing today at which they are successful. Connect to something they'll do tomorrow.

☐ ☐ Stop all activities 15 to 30 minutes before the bell/signal to leave the room so there is time for closing activities. Leave time for reflection. Have students pick up and clean up the room. Check: What can we look forward to doing tomorrow? Check: What is tonight's homework assignment? Check: What did you learn today? Finally, have students practice lining up for leaving the room. One practice run should suffice. Reteach this if it is not flawlessly done! Prepare students for the bell so that when it rings, they will line up flawlessly the very first time.

☺ Smile! You did it!

Notes:

_____

_____

_____

_____

_____

_____

_____

_____

_____

_____

_____

_____

Reflective Practice for Better Teaching

Reflection is thinking in a systematic way about what has taken place and what should take place next. Reflection precedes and follows instruction, back and forth, in a continuous loop. Reflection frames questions like, "What went well? What did not? What needs to change? How can it be better next time?" In contemporary U.S. schools, time for teacher reflection is rare. Even if time were provided for so gentle an activity as reflection, some louder priority would be sure to push it aside. With so many pressures and stresses on teachers, the sheer busyness of the school day limits opportunities to think about what has taken place. Nevertheless, reflection is fundamental to change, and should take place *somewhere* and at *some point in time.* Try to find a time and place for reflection one step better than while sitting in heavy traffic on your way home, or riding the subway half asleep in the morning! If we are to become the best teachers we can be, we must work to continually improve both our teaching skills and our skill in creating a positive classroom.

In his synthesis of research identifying teacher behaviors that contribute to student achievement, James H. Stronge emphasizes the importance of reflection, which "has been described repeatedly in studies of teacher effectiveness" (2002, p. 20). Stronge adds that reflective teachers are "students of learning," saying:

> They are curious about the art and science of teaching and about themselves as effective teachers. They constantly improve lessons, think about how to reach particular students, and seek and try out new approaches in the classroom to better meet the needs of their learners. (p. 21)

Reflection drives our growth as teachers. It guides us toward improvement, toward doing something better than we have done it previously. As an inner-city classroom teacher, I constantly asked myself, "How can I do a better job teaching these students? What technique worked? What idea did not work out at all?" These reflections opened me to trying something new or doing something differently.

Trying is the main word here. To be most helpful, reflection has to involve more than words; it must result in action. Some actual change must follow reflection, or else reflection is an exercise in good intentions. When teaching, I would write a note reminding myself to do something the next day, clip it to my daily planner, and keep it right on my desk as a reminder: "Don't give out work sheets until directions are clear," or, "Anna and Steffan—call on them to participate!"

THE SCHOOL-YEAR CYCLES OF REFLECTION: IMMEDIATE AND COMPREHENSIVE

Research and common sense tell us that self-evaluation is best when it is systematic. *Systematic* means that you do it regularly—after teaching a new lesson, for instance, or at the end of a school day. After instruction, we informally reflect on what went well and what did not work well. During the course of the school year (and even during holiday periods), teachers should continually reflect.

Effective teachers report that two types of reflection are necessary: immediate and comprehensive. Immediate reflection is looking back over the day, week, or month and asking yourself what went well, what did not, and what you are going to do about it. Comprehensive reflection is more structured—it involves listing the spiritual, physical, instructional, and managerial tasks and evaluating how well you are achieving each. Let's look first at how to do immediate reflections.

Immediate Reflection

There are four times during the school year when it is best to do an immediate reflection:

1. At the end of the first day

2. At the end of the first week

3. During the last week of December (or, if your school is on a year-round schedule, during the last week of the school year's fourth month)

4. At the end of the school year

The following is an outline for immediate reflection:

AT END OF FIRST DAY

What went well:

Proof:

What did not:

Proof:

Action (What I MUST change for tomorrow):

At the end of my first day of teaching, my immediate reflection outline looked something like this:

AT END OF FIRST DAY

What went well: *I established a safe climate in the class. The students are looking forward to tomorrow. They like me. Whew!*

Proof: *During our group discussion all students participated, and this cooperation seemed to carry over to recess. They also felt comfortable with the new routines.*

What did not: *Math lesson bombed.*

Proof: *I rushed through the lesson. Many of the students did not understand the concepts. They looked puzzled and had many questions I didn't have time to address.*

Action (What I MUST change for tomorrow): *Slow down. Cut down amount of content I want to cover. Allow more time for student questions.*

At the end of your very first week of teaching, do your second immediate reflection. Follow the same simple format:

AT END OF FIRST WEEK

What went well:

Proof:

What did not:

Proof:

Action (What I MUST change for Monday):

As with your first immediate reflection, select a few items for "What went well," but select only one item for "What did not." If you choose more than one, you will lose focus, you will become overwhelmed, and most likely you will not make that important change.

Reflection works the same way with classroom management issues. If routines are not smooth (students argue over jobs, make claims of unfairness, etc.), reflect. Take that reflection and follow it up with action.

Following is what my first week looked like:

AT END OF FIRST WEEK

What went well: *Most things are going well. Students seem to like me. Vocabulary words are challenging.*

Proof: *Students are doing their homework. Classwork seems to be done on time. Ginny brought me part of her lunch after I said how I was "always hungry"!*

What did not: *Noisiness. Misbehavior.*

Proof: *Students fool around too much while I am off working with other reading groups.*

Action (What I MUST change for Monday): *Make sure they understand I am working with other groups and cannot share my attention during those times. Talk to them about the importance of quiet during reading group time.*

At the end of my first week teaching, my immediate reflection told me that on the whole, things were going well, but there were trouble spots starting to appear. In fact, this "action" that I took did not solve the problem as well as I had hoped. "Talking to them" was important, but it took a later reflection (and input from a valued colleague) to really get a handle on the disruption during reading group time.

Following is the format (same as before) for the third immediate reflection:

AT END OF DECEMBER

What went well:

Proof:

What did not:

Proof:

Action (What I MUST change for the new year):

By the school break in December I was exhausted. The "What did not" work was still my reading groups: No matter how much I talked to them and got steamed, it seemed to do no good. I asked the teacher next door to come in and observe. He graciously gave up two of his free preparation periods to do so. We sat in the teacher's room afterward, and he helped me plan my action for January, encouraging me that it was not too late for a fresh start.

To him, the proof was obvious: My most disruptive students were those who finished early. They had nothing to do, so they started quietly fooling around, then yelling, then physically pushing each other to the point where I had to intervene.

The remedy my neighbor teacher recommended was my assigning work that was (a) sufficiently challenging—no easy baby work in reading—and (b) sufficiently lengthy so that my students would not be done in 5 minutes. It had to be meaningful and complex. In addition, the students had to have something concrete to do—on their own—once they finished their reading group work, as well as a clear one-to-one message that they were to stay on task.

On the following pages I provide four immediate reflection work sheets. Use each work sheet to focus your reflections at each of the four immediate reflection points (at the end of the first day, at the end of the first week, during the fourth week of December, and at the end of the school year). Remember: If your circumstances are particularly difficult (as mine became), get help with your reflections. Locate a colleague, or a nonjudgmental administrator with teaching experience, to sit and review your reflections with you. (This reflection should be an adult activity, but don't hesitate to include evidence from your students to support or contradict your reflections.) Brainstorm to come up with an action plan. Redraw your earlier action plan, if necessary. Work short term— look toward tomorrow, and come up with action for tomorrow. Work on only one problem at a time; start with your biggest or most pressing one. Do not allow yourself to be overwhelmed. Get yourself through one day before you start planning for a week or a month at a time, but do not ignore problems you are experiencing. They will not go away on their own.

First Immediate Reflection: AT END OF FIRST DAY

What went well:

Proof:

What did not:

Proof:

Action (What I MUST change for TOMORROW):

Second Immediate Reflection: AT END OF FIRST WEEK

What went well:

Proof:

What did not:

Proof:

Action (What I MUST change for MONDAY):

Third Immediate Reflection: AT END OF DECEMBER

What went well:

Proof:

What did not:

Proof:

Action (What I MUST change for the NEW YEAR):

Fourth Immediate Reflection: AT END OF SCHOOL YEAR

What went well:

Proof:

What did not:

Proof:

Action (What I MUST change for THE FIRST DAY OF SCHOOL):

Comprehensive Reflection

In addition to the times for immediate reflection, there are times when a more comprehensive reflection is called for. Immediate reflection looks within ("How did I do today?"), whereas comprehensive reflection asks you to look at each dimension of the positive classroom (spiritual, physical, instructional, and managerial) and reflect: "How well am I addressing practices within each dimension?"

Drawn from the strategies and skills for creating a positive classroom as discussed in Parts I and II, the following comprehensive reflection checklists cover the spiritual, physical, instructional, and managerial dimensions. Consider each as a looking-back and a looking-ahead planning guide. I suggest that you carry out a comprehensive reflection once or twice during the year, perhaps once shortly after the start of school, and again near the end of the school year.

At each time, review each checklist yourself, or have a mentor or trusted colleague go over it with you. Refer back to Parts I or II of this book to refresh your memory. Determine which points need attention. Pick one or two from your "sorta" or "not yet" list, and come up with an action you will take in each case. Write out your plan of action. Bring it to work with you—place it on your teacher's desk. Tape it there and refer to it during the day. Always let your mentor or buddy teacher in on your plan.

COMPREHENSIVE REFLECTION CHECKLISTS

	okay ☺	sorta ☺	not yet ☹

Spiritual Checklist

	okay	sorta	not yet
1. Have I discussed basic understandings with my students?	☐	☐	☐
2. Do I make eye contact when speaking with my students?	☐	☐	☐
3. Do my students feel they are heard?	☐	☐	☐
4. Do students enjoy being in my class?	☐	☐	☐
5. Do I clearly communicate instructional expectations?	☐	☐	☐
6. Do I convey enthusiasm?	☐	☐	☐
7. Do I hold students accountable?	☐	☐	☐
8. Are my students aware of their attributions?	☐	☐	☐
9. Have all my students experienced at least some success?	☐	☐	☐
10. Do I treat my students like individuals?	☐	☐	☐
11. Do my students know how to resolve basic conflicts on their own?	☐	☐	☐
12. Is empathic behavior openly valued?	☐	☐	☐
13. Have I given up red pens/pencils?	☐	☐	☐

Physical Checklist

	okay	sorta	not yet
1. Are the "nuts and bolts" in place?	☐	☐	☐
2. Is the "human factor" working well?	☐	☐	☐
3. Does my classroom feel like a safe and pleasant place to be?	☐	☐	☐
4. Does my classroom allow for symbolic identification?	☐	☐	☐
5. Does my classroom allow for corrective interventions?	☐	☐	☐

Instructional Checklist

As I teach:

	okay	sorta	not yet
1. Am I aware of and using the eight key teaching skills?	☐	☐	☐
2. Do I convey instructional expectations?	☐	☐	☐
3. Are students kept accountable for their work?	☐	☐	☐
4. Are my students successful in academics?	☐	☐	☐

Use of strategies:

	okay	sorta	not yet
1. Do I teach at the right level of difficulty?	☐	☐	☐
2. Do I break instruction into smaller learnings?	☐	☐	☐

	okay ☺	sorta ☺	not yet ☹
3. Do I use patterning or association in each lesson?	☐	☐	☐
4. Is adequate time provided?	☐	☐	☐
5. Does my teaching encourage cooperation?	☐	☐	☐
6. Do I have a sense of students' nonacademic strengths?	☐	☐	☐
7. Are students taking responsibility for their learning?	☐	☐	☐
8. Are students interested in their work?	☐	☐	☐
9. Do I provide continuous (formative) assessment?	☐	☐	☐
10. Do I make use of informal assessments?	☐	☐	☐
11. Is my instruction flow smooth?	☐	☐	☐
12. Is my pacing about right?	☐	☐	☐

Managerial Checklist

Before the fact, do I:

1. Understand school procedures and policies?	☐	☐	☐
2. Know my students' past school life and history?	☐	☐	☐
3. Know my students' interests?	☐	☐	☐
4. Know my students' special needs?	☐	☐	☐
5. Make sure all students know the routines and procedures for the classroom?	☐	☐	☐
6. Make limits clear?	☐	☐	☐

During the fact, do I:

1. Model desired behavior?	☐	☐	☐
2. Move around and make eye contact?	☐	☐	☐
3. Discuss students' attributions?	☐	☐	☐
4. Go lightly on rewards and persuading?	☐	☐	☐
5. Smile?	☐	☐	☐

When faced with misbehavior, do I:

1. Keep things moving?	☐	☐	☐
2. Identify and deal with the misbehavior quickly and easily?	☐	☐	☐
3. Maintain dignity—mine and the students'?	☐	☐	☐

When my responses are called for, do I use:

1. Nonresponses?	☐	☐	☐
2. Signal responses?	☐	☐	☐

	okay ☺	sorta 😐	not yet ☹
3. Physical closeness responses?	☐	☐	☐
4. Humor responses?	☐	☐	☐
5. Private verbal responses?	☐	☐	☐

Do I avoid:

	okay	sorta	not yet
1. Harsh, public responses?	☐	☐	☐
2. Punitive physical responses?	☐	☐	☐

When faced with particularly serious problem behaviors, which of these strategies have I used?

	okay	sorta	not yet
1. Talking to student; use of "I" messages	☐	☐	☐
2. Denial of classroom privileges	☐	☐	☐
3. Exclusion from class	☐	☐	☐
4. Student reflective activities	☐	☐	☐
5. Prosocial detention	☐	☐	☐
6. Parental involvement	☐	☐	☐
7. Daily (or weekly) report card	☐	☐	☐
8. Self-instruction strategies	☐	☐	☐
9. Contracts	☐	☐	☐
10. Involving the principal and/or other professionals	☐	☐	☐

If faced with a potentially harmful situation, did I (or will I):

	okay	sorta	not yet
Restrain myself from striking a student?	☐	☐	☐
Seek help?	☐	☐	☐
Avoid rash reaction, waiting for calm before proceeding?	☐	☐	☐

Notes:

_____

_____

_____

_____

_____

_____

_____

_____

_____

_____

_____

_____

_____

_____

Conclusion

Being Your Own Best Teacher

I would not want to see myself in action in my first year of teaching. (Thankfully, no such videotape exists!) No, I did not hurt any kids; I did no damage. I worked really hard at teaching (too hard), but I was far from being the best teacher I could be. I wasted time, and my classroom management skills relied heavily on personality—I wanted the students to like me. After all, I liked them, didn't I? So it was a real shock when students—whom I liked—started acting up, acting out, and making my life as a new and inexperienced teacher miserable. I took misbehavior personally. In retrospect, it was an incredibly valuable learning experience (for me if not for them!). In fact, I believe that the first few years of teaching are when a teacher truly learns how to teach. It does not happen in college, nor does it come in student teaching. These are important preparations, but only in setting a foundation. *We learn to teach by teaching.* We learn to create and maintain positive classrooms by doing, not by talking about doing.

As I said earlier, my Aunt Flora was my godmother, my role model, and the one who inspired me to become a teacher. After my first year of teaching, however, I needed more than inspiration to make it work. Frustrated and close to quitting, I desperately needed concrete feedback from my colleagues. I would invite them—*beg* them—to come into my room during their free period and observe me. I had a million questions: Why was I having trouble with classroom behavior? What was I doing wrong? Was I too easy? Too strict? What could they suggest to help me? They not only gave me feedback on my teaching, but they also invited me into their rooms. I saw—and then imitated—strategies they shared and activities that worked with the same tough, inner-city children I taught. Watching them in action was a very powerful boost, leading to a series of "Aha!" moments. I noted the things they did that I wanted to try out on my own.

By my third and fourth years of teaching, I can in all modesty say I was much better. By my fifth year I was awarded tenure. My students' math and reading test scores were up, but I valued more how well my students were able to take responsibility for their behavior. I remember one tough sixth-grade class in particular, filled with kids who had spent years joyfully disobeying lists of rules. Since I still had some "attractive power" (which all new teachers have during the first week or so of school), I focused attention on the basic understanding of respect in our classroom. Pushing aside the books, I explained that I expected them to respect other people. I expected them to also respect themselves. This was nonnegotiable. I devoted a great deal of class time to discussing what the limits of respect were (for instance, students should not take things from others' desks without permission). I drew from students what they thought the elements of respect were (such as teachers not making you feel small if you did not do well on a test or forgot your homework). We spent a lot of time articulating examples of respect the first 2 weeks of school.

Following is a dialogue from my sixth-grade class:

"Mr. D, the problem with teachers is that they don't respect kids."

"Yeah. Teachers want respect, but some of them don't deserve it."

"Carlos, how can a teacher deserve respect?"

"By being nice to people."

"Maritza, how could I act like I respect students? Do I?"

"Easy, Mr. D. You trust us, and don't accuse us all the time of doing things we didn't do. Like Mr. Loftin last year. Nothing we ever did was right. He blamed me for everything—taking his pen, breaking his stapler—everything."

"He had favorites, too."

"So it sounds like respect means caring about people's feelings."

"Yeah. If a teacher acts cool, he'll get respected."

"Okay. Let me tell you a real incident: Once I saw a pencil fall on the floor and the student who picked it up—I'll call him Jack—said it was his. When Maria asked him to give it to her, Jack refused. He said, 'Finders keepers, man. Finders keepers.'"

"Maybe Jack didn't know whose it was."

"But if Maria said it was hers, what should Jack have done?"

"He should ask another person, because maybe she's lying."

"He could do that. But remember respect? What's the respectful thing for Jack to do? Isabella?"

"Mr. D, maybe you should have just made him give the pencil to Maria."

"Do you think that would work? Jacob, what do you think?"

"Hmmm. Maybe not. If you have to get a teacher to force Jack, I don't think that's a good idea either."

"Emma, what do you think?"

"Why can't Jack just believe that Maria is telling the truth, and not think that everyone always lies to get what they want? I don't lie just to get what I want."

The key was that in addition to talking about respect, we practiced it. I led students in practicing how to work together in cooperative groups, how to gather for lunch, how to borrow a pencil from another, and how to ask a question in class. We spent a lot of time going over these matters. It was only then that we could return our attention to academic matters.

With the basic understanding of respect for self and others as common ground, students will grow more reflective and less focused on getting away with things. Students develop their EQ, their intrapersonal and interpersonal intelligences, and their social skills as they are able to generalize respect to other situations, situations for which no explicit rules exist. They will not need huge "School Rules" signs, because they have internalized respect for the environment and can carry it outside the boundary of the classroom. When I took my sixth-grade class on field trips, they would receive compliments on their courtesy and good behavior. Yes, before the trip we talked—about where we would go, what we would see and do, and what the expectations were for safety and behavior. I never had to threaten them or recite a litany of new rules for being out in public, for if throwing trash on our classroom floor was not something neat students like mine did, then neither was throwing trash on the floor of the New York City subway car, or on the floor of the greenhouse at the Brooklyn Botanical Garden. My students had internalized the attribution that they were neat people, aware of their surroundings.

When we returned, I told them I couldn't wait to plan our next class trip. They were the best sixth-grade class I'd ever had. I had never had a more mature group. I told them how lucky I felt being their teacher. They were a little embarrassed, but it empowered them; it taught them that they were capable and good people worthy of others' respect and love. I wasn't really praising them; I was simply saying what I saw them to be.

I expect that my now-adult students use a wastebasket to this very day. And open doors for others.

And say "Thank you."

And . . .

Who knows where our influence ends?

One of my very first students (whom I will call "José") engaged in annoying and antisocial behavior. Other students and teachers seemed to avoid him. His mother tried hard, but José displayed quite troublesome behavior at home as well. For the school's nonexistent music program, I purchased black plastic song flutes out of my own pocket so my fourth-grade students could learn scales and some simple tunes. José took to the song flutes instantly. Although his reading and math scores were way below grade level, he seemed to pick up sight reading and the fingering instantly. I would let him solo for the class on occasion.

Several years later on a visit to New York City, I ran into José's mother. She greeted me warmly and told me that José had been selected to play first clarinet in New York City's All-City Orchestra, comprised of the public school system's best student musicians. I was thrilled to hear the news. Since that day, José's success has served to remind me that all students have potential and real strengths and, if given good guidance and direction that touch upon those strengths, will be able to use that support in a productive way.

In summary: Before we can hope to teach students anything, we have to first create a secure learning environment for them. This means that we must use our power wisely to create and maintain a positive classroom. That positive classroom starts with considering its spiritual, physical, instructional, and managerial dimensions. Within these, preparing and reflecting are the key actions we need to do.

Perhaps the most significant turning point in my teaching career was when I brought my students into the process of their own learning. Once I was secure as a teacher, I could safely look at what my students' needs really were, and not simply at what I or the school district or anyone else needed or thought the students' needs were. Less concerned that disciplinary problems would sabotage my teaching day, I began to listen, to hear my students' words and feelings, individually and as a group. I finally could step outside myself and meet my students, enjoying who they were, where they were, and where they wanted to go. I learned that I did not always have to stand at the front of the line in order to lead. By watching and listening, I could see where they were going and help them lead by walking behind the line. It was more than okay for me to follow them in their journey.

In fact, it was essential that I did so.

Even if you are the most experienced of teachers, you must continue to find out about your students. Look for their strengths, and affirm them clearly to each one. Capitalize on those strengths; create opportunities for each student to have a chance to shine. Realize that there is no better way to win the approval and support of parents than by having them see their children experience success in your classroom. Yes, it is that simple.

The basics and the test scores are important, but for each student you must also promote the value of achievements other than reading, writing, and mathematics. When you teach, ask questions that will arouse curiosity. Ask questions that will allow students to be successful, even if it is within the merest act of answering a question correctly. Empower students to ask the really important questions. Let your students teach you what they know, and where they are headed.

Teaching is a tough job, but the rewards for a job well done are without equal in any other profession. Through preparation, reflection, and a willingness to do, you will become both *your own best teacher* and the best teacher you can be!

Our society needs it desperately.

Resource: Positive Classroom Matrix

The matrix on the following page helps teachers see the big picture of teaching by permitting a deeper look into the organization and structure of positive classrooms. This matrix shows the relationship between three types and times of intervention and the four dimensions of positive classrooms. Preventive and supportive interventions are preferred, since they are proactive and more fruitful. Corrective interventions, although sometimes necessary, are reactive and less constructive.

Dimension of Classroom Management

Type and time of intervention	Spiritual	Physical	Instructional	Managerial
Preventive (before/pre-acting)	Planning for all students to experience success and to feel loved and accepted	Inviting classroom; positive classroom ambience and climate	Preparation; lesson planning; long-range planning	Basic classroom procedures; conflict-resolution plan; limit setting
Supportive (during/acting)	Accepting body language; active listening; eye contact; proximity	Cooperative group seating; prominent display of student work, shared ownership of classroom	Use of effective instructional skills and strategies; encouragement; maintaining momentum	Attribution teaching; teacher and students model positive behavior; teacher movement (eye contact, proximity, gestures)
Corrective (after/reacting)	Providing clear ways for students to "come back"	Use of time-out area; placement of student in quiet, private area within or outside classroom	Instructional contracts; one-to-one instruction; tutorials	Desist strategies; self-instruction strategies; exclusion from class

References

Armstrong, T. (2000). *Multiple intelligences in the classroom* (2nd ed.). Alexandria, VA: Association for Supervision and Curriculum Development.

Balikci, A. (1970). *The Netsilik Eskimo.* Garden City, NY: The Natural History Press.

ben Shea, N., & Di Giulio, R. C. (2005). *A compass for the classroom: How teachers (and students) can find their way & keep from getting lost.* Thousand Oaks, CA: Corwin Press.

Bryan, J., & Walbek, N. (1970). Preaching and practicing generosity: Children's actions and reactions. *Child Development, 41,* 329–353.

Buka, S., & Earls, F. (1993). Early determinants of delinquency and violence. *Health Affairs, 12*(2), 46–64.

Carlson, M. O., Humphrey, G. E., & Reinhardt, K. S. (2003). *Weaving science inquiry and continuous assessment.* Thousand Oaks, CA: Corwin Press.

Center on Juvenile and Criminal Justice. (2002). *School house hype: Two years later.* Retrieved September 1, 2006, from http://www.cjcj.org/pubs/schoolhouse/shh2.html

Di Giulio, R. (1978, April). The "guaranteed" behavior improvement plan. *Teacher,* pp. 22–26.

Di Giulio, R. (1994). *Successful Vermont teachers describe their classroom practices.* Unpublished manuscript, Johnson State College, Vermont.

Di Giulio, R. (2004). *Great teaching: What matters most in helping students succeed.* Thousand Oaks, CA: Corwin Press.

Durkheim, E. (1961). *Moral education* (I. K. Wilson & H. Schnurer, Trans.). New York: Free Press. (Original work published 1925)

Erikson, E. H. (1963). *Childhood and society* (2nd ed.). New York: Norton.

Fliegel, S. (1993). *Miracle in East Harlem.* New York: Times Books.

Gardner, H. (1983). *Frames of mind.* New York: Basic Books.

Gardner, H. (1993). *Multiple intelligences: The theory in practice.* New York: Basic Books.

Gettinger, M. (1995). Best practices for increasing academic learning time. In A. Thomas & J. Grimes (Eds.), *Best practice in school psychology* (Vol. 3, pp. 943–954). Washington, DC: National Association of School Psychologists.

Gettinger, M., & Stoiber, K. C. (1999). Excellence in teaching: Review of instructional and environmental variables. In C. R. Reynolds & T. B. Gutkin (Eds.), *The handbook of school psychology* (3rd ed., pp. 933–958). New York: Wiley.

Goleman, D. (1995). *Emotional intelligence: Why it can matter more than IQ.* New York: Bantam.

Gotham Gazette. (2003, April 7). *Teachers who quit.* Retrieved May 15, 2006, from http://www.gothamgazette.com/article//20030407/202/339

Greene, L. J. (2005). *Helping students fix problems and avoid crises.* Thousand Oaks, CA: Corwin Press.

Hartshorne, H., & May, M. (1930). *Studies in deceit.* New York: Macmillan.

Hyman, I., & Perone, D. (1998). The other side of school violence: Educator policies and practices that may contribute to student misbehavior. *Journal of School Psychology, 36*(1), 7–27.

Joubert, J. (1928). *Pensees and letters of Joseph Joubert* (H. Collins, Ed. and Trans.). New York: Brentano's.

Kamii, K. K., & DeClark, G. (1985). *Young children reinvent arithmetic: Implications of Piaget's theory.* New York: Teachers College Press.

Kohn, A. (1993a). Choices for children: Why and how to let students decide. *Phi Delta Kappan, 75,* 8–20.

Kohn, A. (1993b). Rewards versus learning: A response to Paul Chance. *Phi Delta Kappan, 73,* 783–787.

Kohn, A. (1995). *Punished by rewards.* Boston: Houghton Mifflin.

Marzano, R. J., & Marzano, J. S. (2006). The key to classroom management. In B. A. Marlowe & A. S. Canestrari (Eds.), *Educational psychology in context: Readings for future teachers* (pp. 24–39). Thousand Oaks, CA: Sage Publications.

Maslow, A. (1970). *Motivation and personality.* New York: Harper & Row.

McLuhan, M., & Fiore, Q. (1967). *The medium is the massage: An inventory of effects.* New York: Bantam.

Metropolitan Life Insurance Company. (1993). *The Metropolitan Life survey of the American teacher 1993: Violence in America's public schools.* New York: Author.

Murray, W. (1994, July/August). Have we got a design for you! *Instructor,* pp. 59–62.

Musca, T. (Producer/Writer), & Menéndez, R. (Writer/Director). (1988). *Stand and deliver* [Motion picture]. United States: Warner Bro. Pictures.

National Center on Educational Restructuring and Inclusion. (1995). *National study on inclusive education.* New York City University of New York Press.

New Hampshire Board of Education. (1853). *Seventh annual report upon the common schools of New Hampshire.* Concord, NH: Butterfield & Hill.

Noguera, P. A. (1995). Preventing and producing violence: A critical analysis of responses to school violence. *Harvard Educational Review, 65*(2), 206.

Perez, S. (2000). An ethic of caring in teaching culturally diverse students. *Education, 121,* 102–105.

Pew Research Center for the People & the Press. (2005, April 19). *Support for tougher indecency measures, but worries about government intrusiveness: New concerns about Internet and reality shows.* Retrieved September 1, 2006, from http://people-press.org/reports/display.php3?ReportID=241

Reimer, J., Paolitto, D. P., & Hersh, R. H. (1983). *Promoting moral growth.* New York: Longman.

Rosenshine, B., & Stevens, R. (1986). Teaching functions. In M. C. Wittrock (Ed.), *Handbook of research on teaching: A project of the American Educational Research Association* (pp. 376–391). New York: Simon & Schuster/Macmillan.

Schuster, K. (1997, March 30). School suspends trio. *The New Haven Register,* pp. Al, A8.

Sebok, A. J. (2001, January 15). *New York City's $50 million strip-search suit settlement: How a Fourth Amendment violation became a mass tort lawsuit.* FindLaw Legal Commentary. Retrieved June 13, 2005, from http://writ.news.findlaw.com/scripts/printer_friendly.pl?page=sebok/20010115.html

Seligman, M. E. P. (1975). *Helplessness: On depression, development, and death.* San Francisco: Freeman.

Sergiovanni, T. (1994). *Building community in schools.* San Francisco: Jossey-Bass.

Skiba, R., & Peterson, R. (1999). The dark side of zero tolerance: Can punishment lead to safe schools? *Phi Delta Kappan, 80,* 372–376, 381–382.

Slavin, R. (1990). *Cooperative learning.* Englewood Cliffs, NJ: Prentice Hall.

Slavin, R. (1994). *A practical guide to cooperative learning.* Boston: Allyn & Bacon.

Stanford, B. (1995). Conflict resolution and the story of our lives: Teaching English for violence prevention. *English Journal, 84*(5), 38–42.

Stone, K. F., & Dillehunt, H. Q. (1978). *Self-science: The subject is me.* Santa Monica, CA: Goodyear.

Stronge, J. H. (2002). *Qualities of effective teachers.* Alexandria, VA: Association for Supervision and Curriculum Development.

Tomlinson, C. A. (1999). *The differentiated classroom: Responding to the needs of all learners.* Alexandria, VA: Association for Supervision and Curriculum Development.

Tomlinson, C. A. (2001). *How to differentiate instruction in mixed-ability classrooms.* Alexandria, VA: Association for Supervision and Curriculum Development.

United States Department of Education. (1998, March). *Violence and discipline problems in United States public schools: 1996–1997* (NCES No. 98–030). Washington, DC: National Center for Education Statistics.

United States Department of Education, National Center for Education Statistics. (2004). Elementary and secondary education. In *Digest of education statistics, 2004* (chap. 2). Retrieved September 1, 2006, from http://nces.ed.gov/programs/digest/d04/lt2.asp#c2

United States Department of Justice, Bureau of Justice Statistics. (2005a). *Key crime & justice facts at a glance.* Retrieved April 7, 2006, from http://www.ojp.usdoj.gov/bjs/glance.htm

United States Department of Justice, Bureau of Justice Statistics. (2005b). *Prison statistics.* Retrieved April 7, 2006, from http://usgovinfo.about.com/gi/dynamic/offsite.htm?zi=1/XJ&sdn=usgovinfo&zu=http%3A%2F%2Fwww.ojp.usdoj.gov%2Fbjs%2F

United States Department of Justice, Bureau of Justice Statistics. (2005c). *Serious violent crime levels declined since 1993.* Retrieved April 1, 2006, from www.ojp.usdoj.gov/bjs/glance/cv2.htm

Villa, R. A., & Thousand, J. S. (2006). Is full inclusion of disabled students desirable? In J. W. Noll (Ed.), *Taking sides: Clashing views on controversial educational issues* (13th ed.). Dubuque, Iowa: McGraw-Hill/Dushkin.

Wang, M. C., Haertel, G. D., & Walberg, H. J. (1993/1994). What helps students learn? *Educational Leadership, 51*(4), 74–79.

Wasley, P. A. (2002, February). Small classes, small schools: The time is now. *Educational Leadership,* pp. 6–10.

Whitmire, R. (1994, January 11). Study finds early steps critical to halting violence. *Burlington Free Press,* p. 10A.

Wiggins, G. (2005). *Understanding by design* (2nd ed.). Alexandria, VA: Association for Supervision and Curriculum Development.

Wolfgang, C. H. (2004). *Solving discipline and classroom management problems: Methods and models for today's teachers* (6th ed.). New York: Wiley.

Suggested Reading

Armstrong, T. (2000). *Multiple intelligences in the classroom* (2nd ed.). Alexandria, VA: Association for Supervision and Curriculum Development.

ben Shea, N., & Di Giulio, R. (2004). *A compass for the classroom: How teachers and students can find their way and keep from getting lost.* Thousand Oaks, CA: Corwin Press.

Brubacher, J., Case, C., & Reagan, T. (1999). *Becoming a reflective educator: How to build a culture of inquiry in the schools* (2nd ed.). Thousand Oaks, CA: Corwin Press.

Carlson, M. O., Humphrey, G. E., & Reinhardt, K. S. (2003). *Weaving science inquiry and continuous assessment.* Thousand Oaks, CA: Corwin Press.

DeVries, R., & Zan, B. (1994). *Moral classrooms, moral children: Creating a constructivist atmosphere in early education.* New York: Teachers College Press.

Eisenberg, N., & Mussen, P. (1989). *The roots of prosocial behavior in children.* Cambridge, UK: Cambridge University Press.

Elias, M., & Arnold, H. (2006). *The educator's guide to emotional intelligence and academic achievement.* Thousand Oaks, CA: Corwin Press.

Gardner, H. (1991). *The unschooled mind: How children think and how schools should teach.* New York: Basic Books.

Gardner, H. (1993). *Frames of mind: The theory of multiple intelligences.* New York: Basic Books.

Gentle Teaching International. Retrieved April 1, 2006, from http://www.gentle teaching.com/

Ginott, H. G. (1997). *Teacher and child: A book for parents and teachers.* New York: Simon & Schuster.

Goleman, D. (1995). *Emotional intelligence: Why it can matter more than IQ.* New York: Bantam.

Goleman, D. (1998) *Working with emotional intelligence.* New York: Bantam.

Good, T. L., & Brophy, J. E. (2003). *Looking in classrooms* (9th ed.). Boston: Allyn & Bacon.

Harmin, M. (1994). *Inspiring active learning: A handbook for teachers.* Alexandria, VA: Association for Supervision and Curriculum Development.

Kohn, A. (1996). *Beyond discipline: From compliance to community.* Alexandria, VA: Association for Supervision and Curriculum Development.

Kohn, A. (1999). *Punished by rewards: The trouble with gold stars, incentive plans, A's, praise, and other bribes.* Boston: Houghton Mifflin.

Krishnamurti, J. (1953). *Education and the significance of life.* New York: Harper & Row.

Lightfoot, S. L. (1978). *Worlds apart: Relationships between families and schools.* New York: Basic Books.

Marlowe, B. A., & Page, M. L. (2005). *Creating and sustaining the constructivist classroom.* Thousand Oaks, CA: Corwin Press.

Marzano, R., Marzano, J. S., & Pickering, D. J. (2003). *Classroom management that works: Research-based strategies for every teacher.* Alexandria, VA: Association for Supervision and Curriculum Development

McGee, J. J. (1989). *Being together: Toward a psychology of human interdependence.* Omaha, NE: Creighton University.

McGee, J. J., & Menolascino, F. J. (1991). *Beyond gentle teaching: A non-aversive approach to helping those in need.* New York: Plenum.

Meier, D., & Wood, G. (Eds.). (2004). *Many children left behind: How the No Child Left Behind Act is damaging our children and our schools.* Boston: Beacon Press.

Ohanian, S. (1999). *One size fits few: The folly of educational standards.* Portsmouth, NH: Heinemann.

Smilovitz, R. (1995). *If not now, when? Education, not schooling.* Kearney, NE: Morris.

Wolfgang, C. H. (2005). *Solving discipline and classroom management problems: Methods and models for today's teachers* (6th ed.). New York: Wiley.

Zehm, S., & Kottler, J. (2005). *On being a teacher: The human dimension* (3rd ed.). Thousand Oaks, CA: Corwin Press.

Index

CORWIN PRESS

The Corwin Press logo—a raven striding across an open book—represents the union of courage and learning. Corwin Press is committed to improving education for all learners by publishing books and other professional development resources for those serving the field of PreK–12 education. By providing practical, hands-on materials, Corwin Press continues to carry out the promise of its motto: **"Helping Educators Do Their Work Better."**

CPSIA information can be obtained
at www.ICGtesting.com
Printed in the USA
BVHW080604081222
653662BV00004B/30